Author: Eric Goff

Illustrator: Dave Wolf

Editor: John Fox

Illustrations were created with the ZBrush and Photoshop.

Published in the United States.

Printed in the United States 2020.

ISBN: 978-0-578-85605-6

REPSOULS is a creative company on a mission to honor role models and inspire humanity through thought-provoking animated stories. Chosen role models become inspirations for superhero characters in a new story and 100% of the net profits from book sales are donated to charities they support.

In Liberty's Crown, the honorees were chosen for their humanitarian contributions. They are Barack Obama, Malala Yousafzai, Jimmy Fallon, Ellen DeGeneres, and Elon Musk.

The charities being supported are:

GIRLS OPPORTUNITY ALLIANCE

the ellen fund™
THE ELLEN DEGENERES WILDLIFE FUND

BIG GREEN
REAL FOOD GROWS HERE

MALALA FUND

seriousfun℠
children's network
founded by paul newman

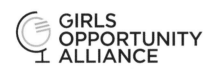

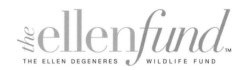

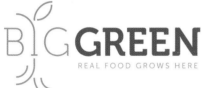

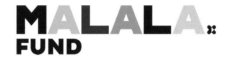

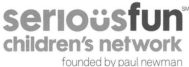

For donation tracking, visit: www.repsouls.com

Disclaimer:

REAL

EXTRAORDINARY

PEOPLE

SUPPORTING

OTHERS &

UPLIFTING

LIVES

SELFLESSLY

REPSOULS
LIBERTY'S CROWN

LET THE STORY BEGIN...

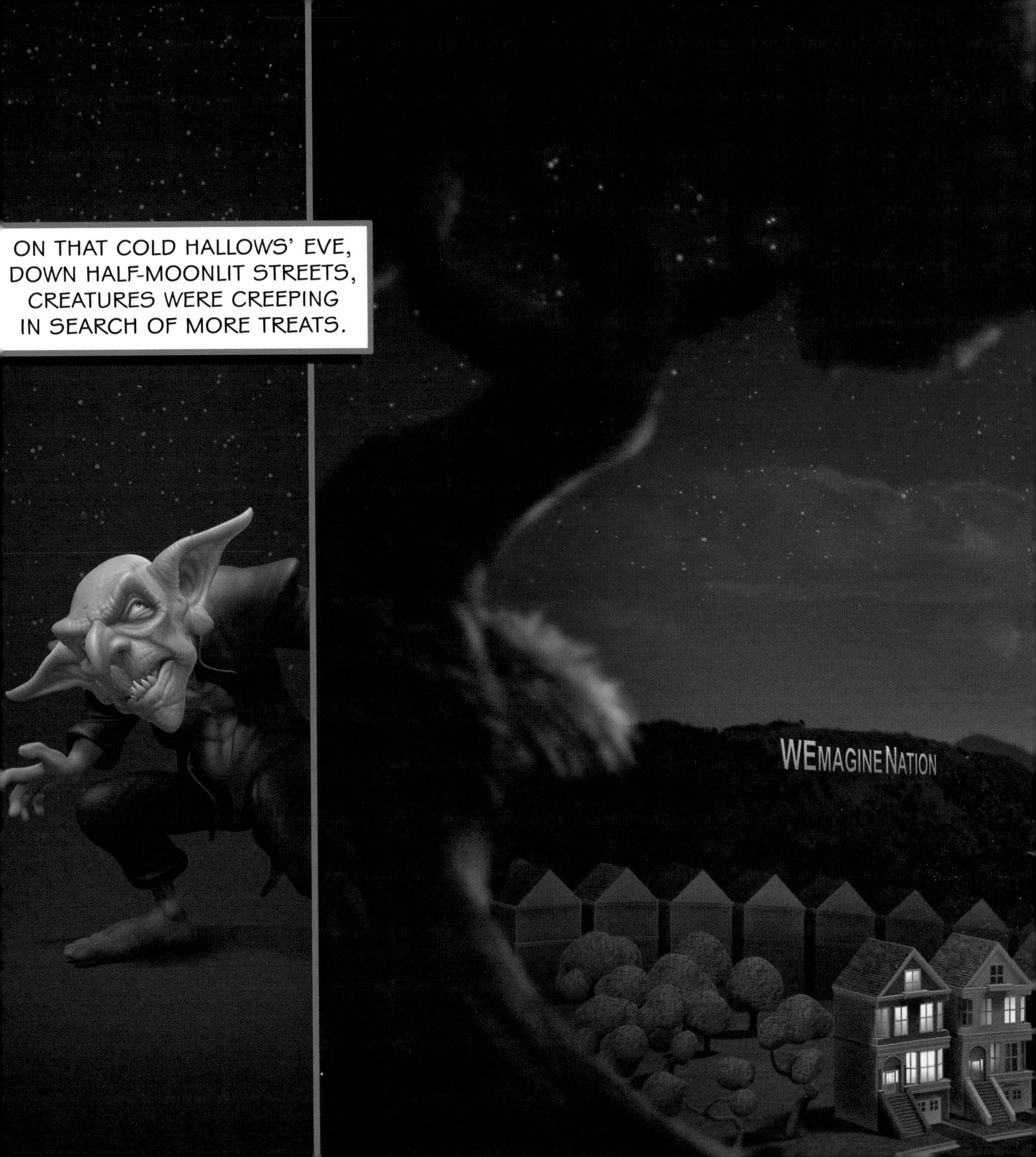
ON THAT COLD HALLOWS' EVE, DOWN HALF-MOONLIT STREETS, CREATURES WERE CREEPING IN SEARCH OF MORE TREATS.
WEMAGINE NATION

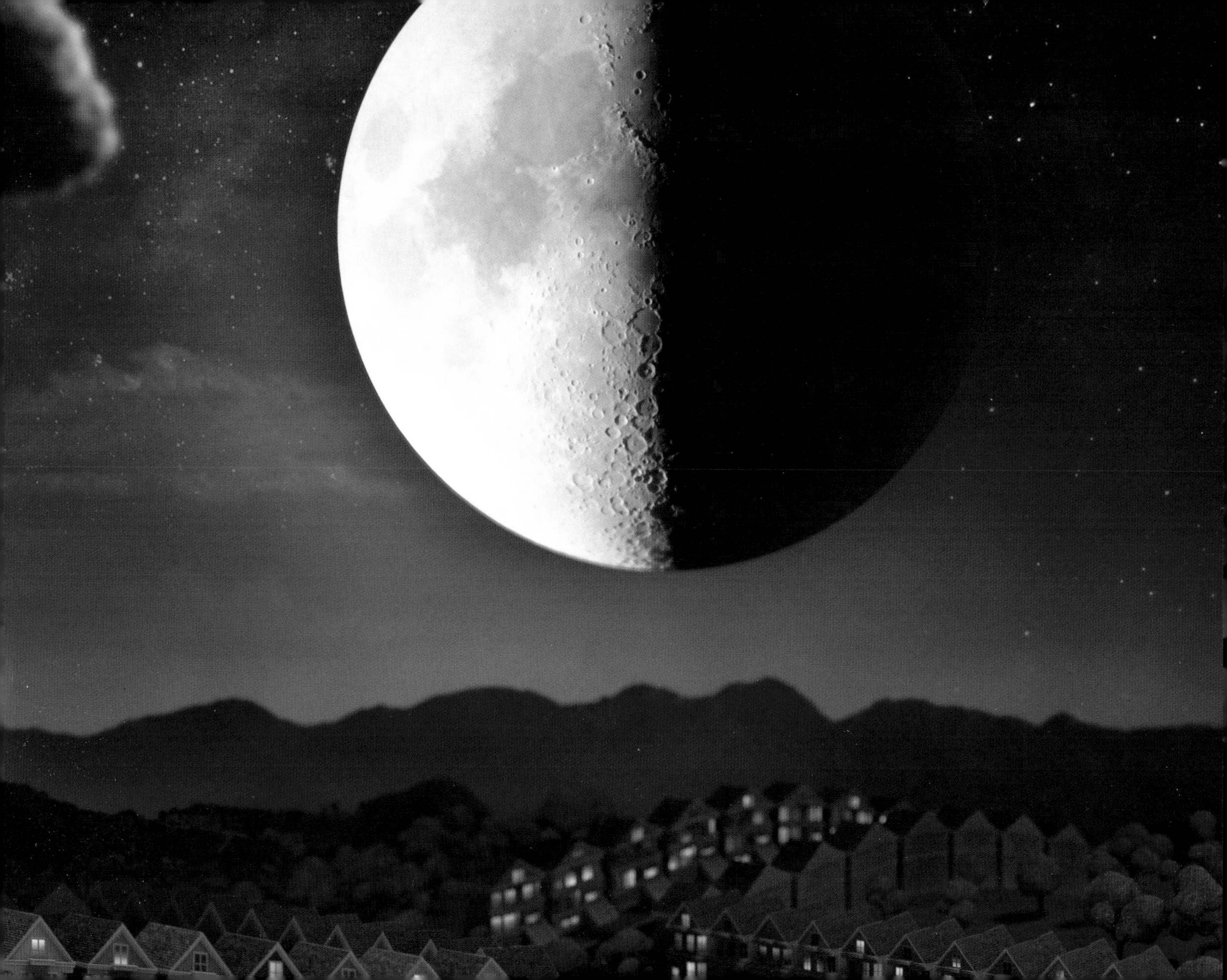

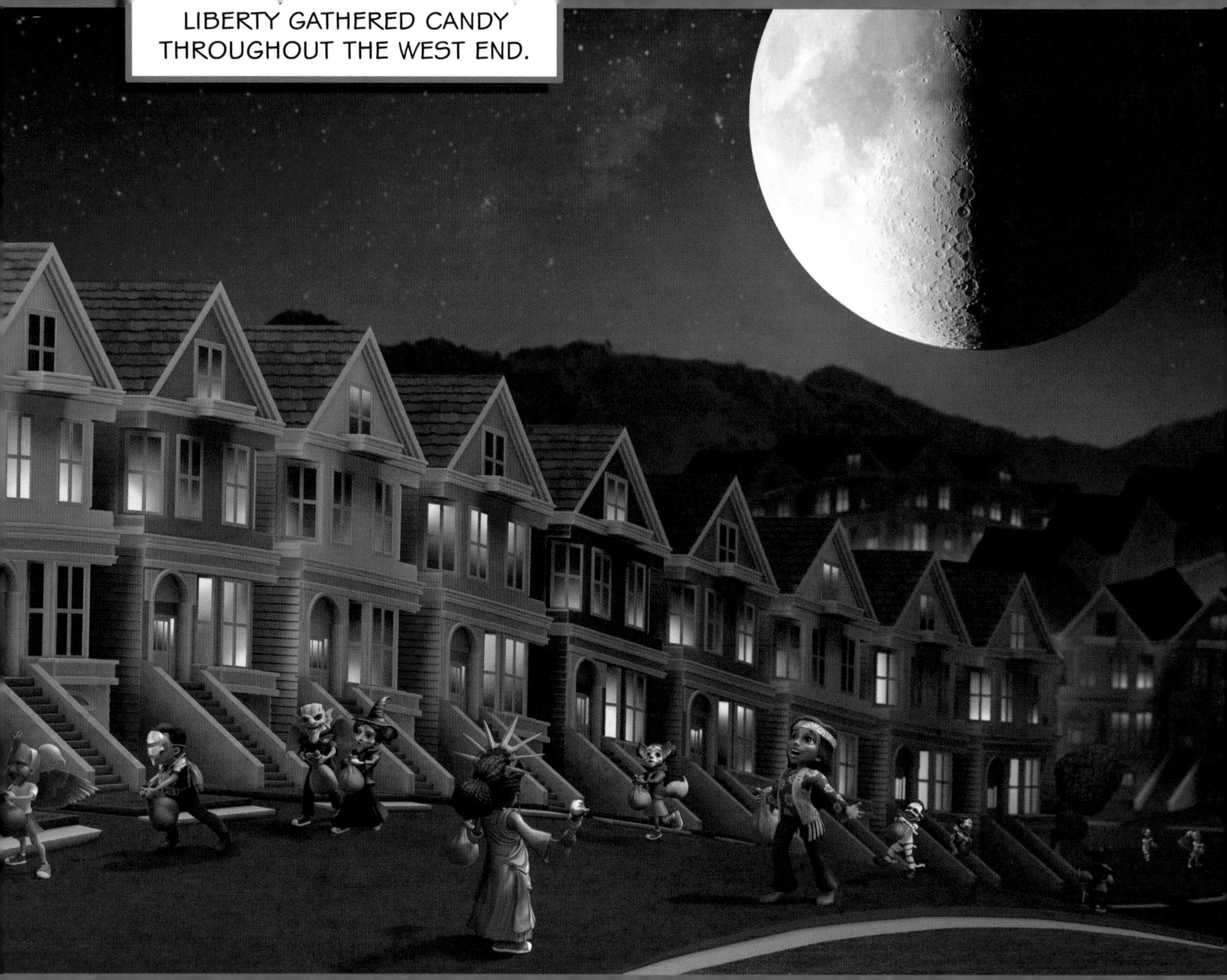
LIBERTY GATHERED CANDY
THROUGHOUT THE WEST END.

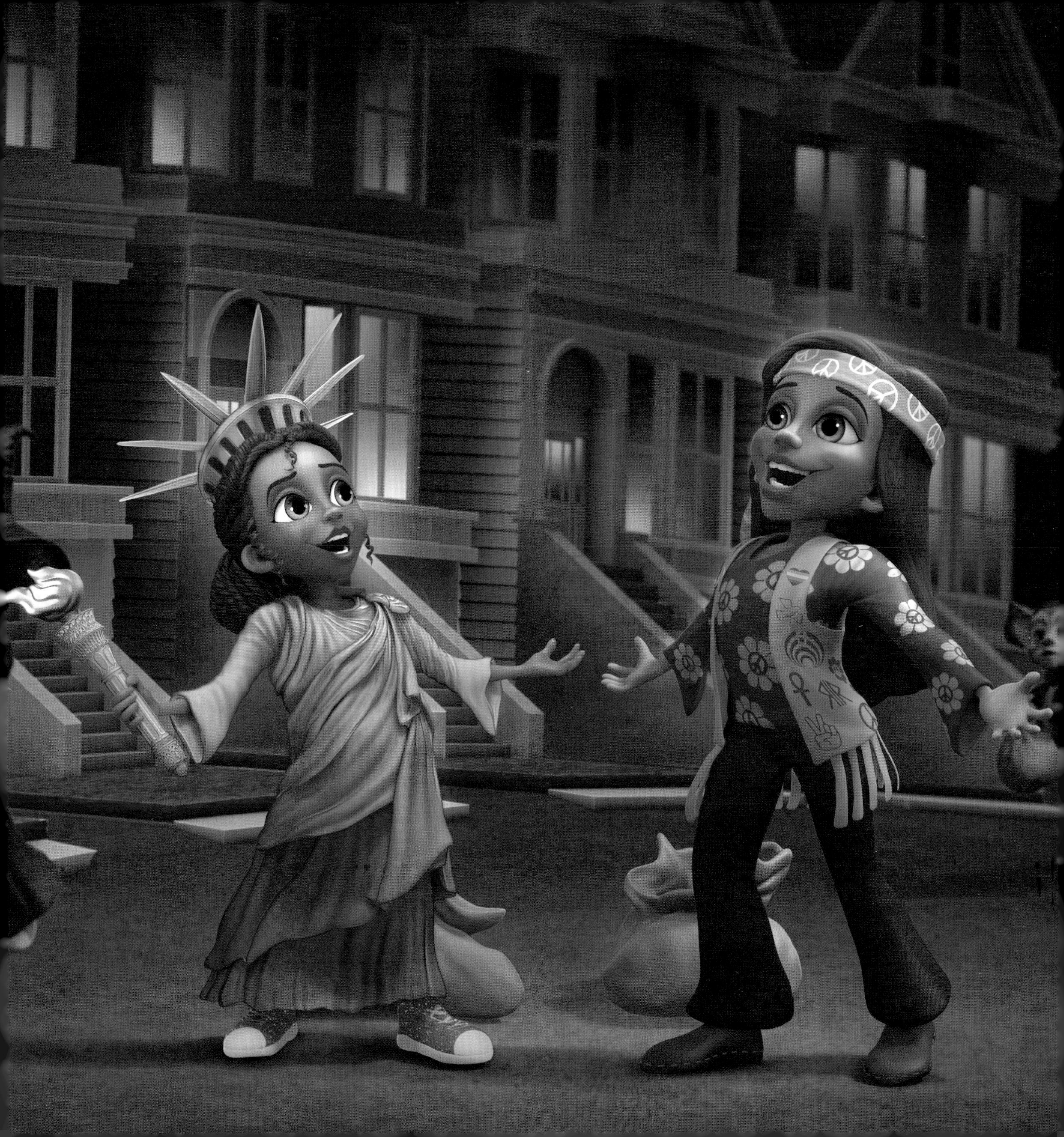

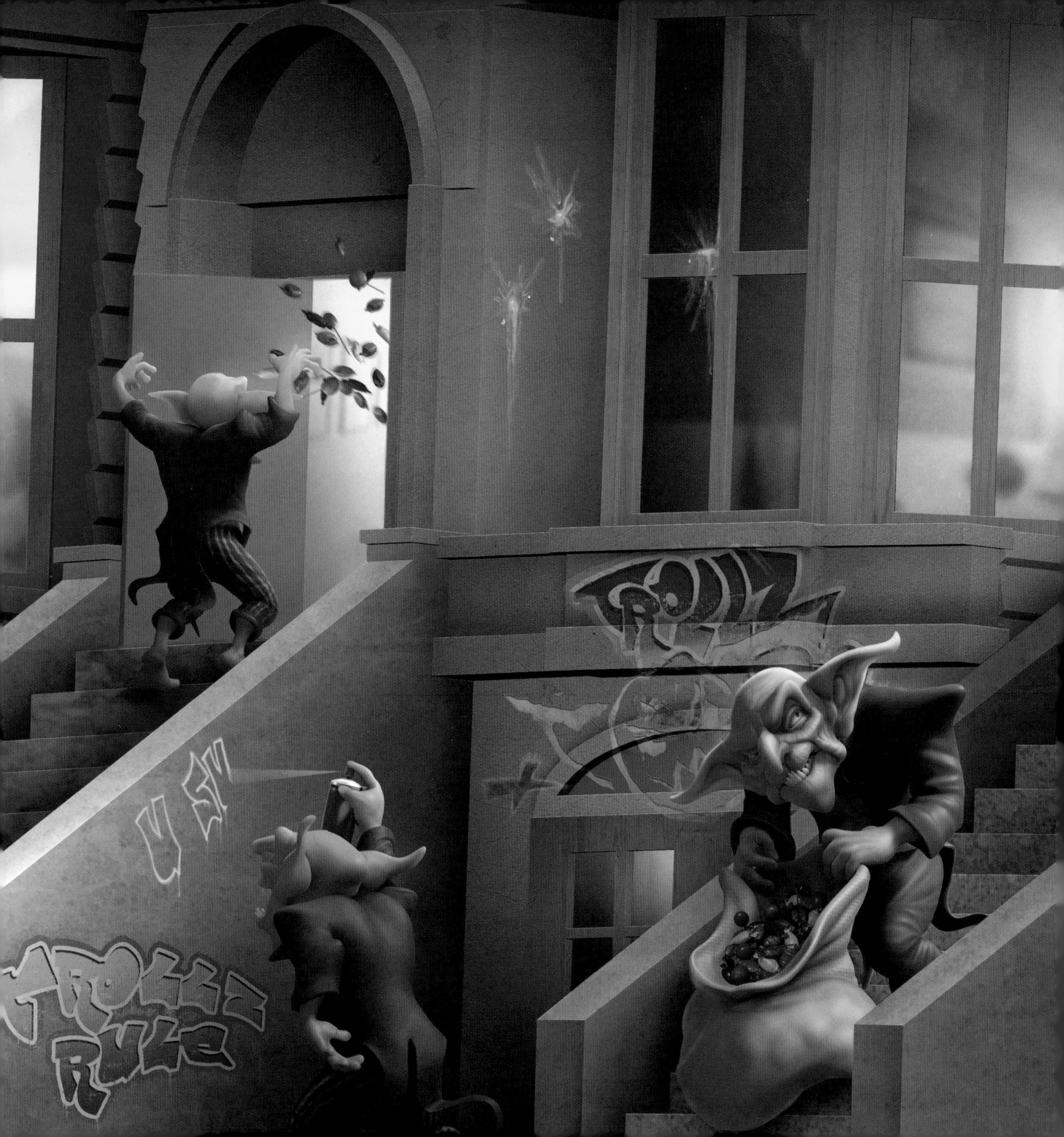
TROLLZ
RULE

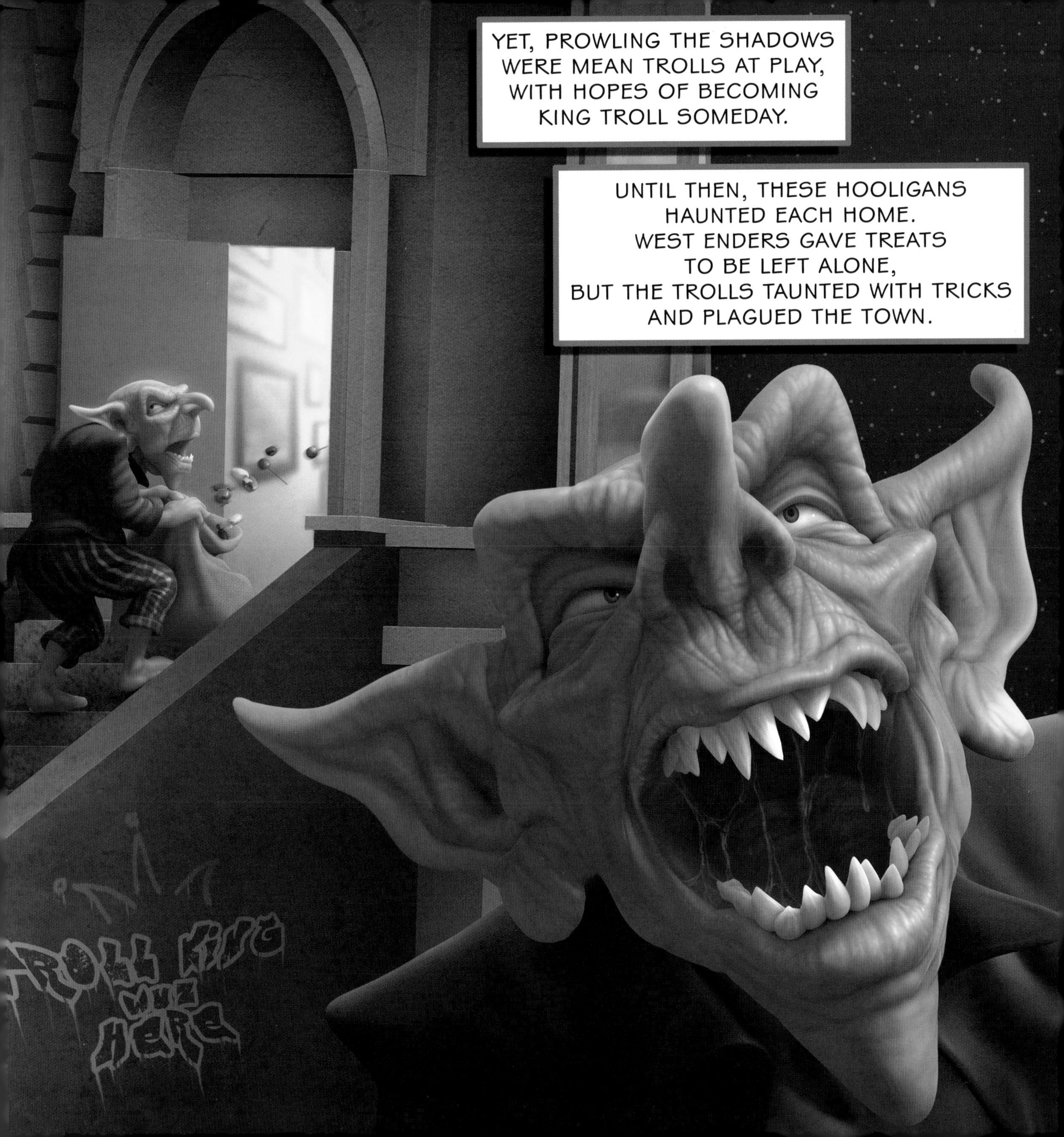
YET, PROWLING THE SHADOWS
WERE MEAN TROLLS AT PLAY,
WITH HOPES OF BECOMING
KING TROLL SOMEDAY.
UNTIL THEN, THESE HOOLIGANS
HAUNTED EACH HOME.
WEST ENDERS GAVE TREATS
TO BE LEFT ALONE,
BUT THE TROLLS TAUNTED WITH TRICKS
AND PLAGUED THE TOWN.

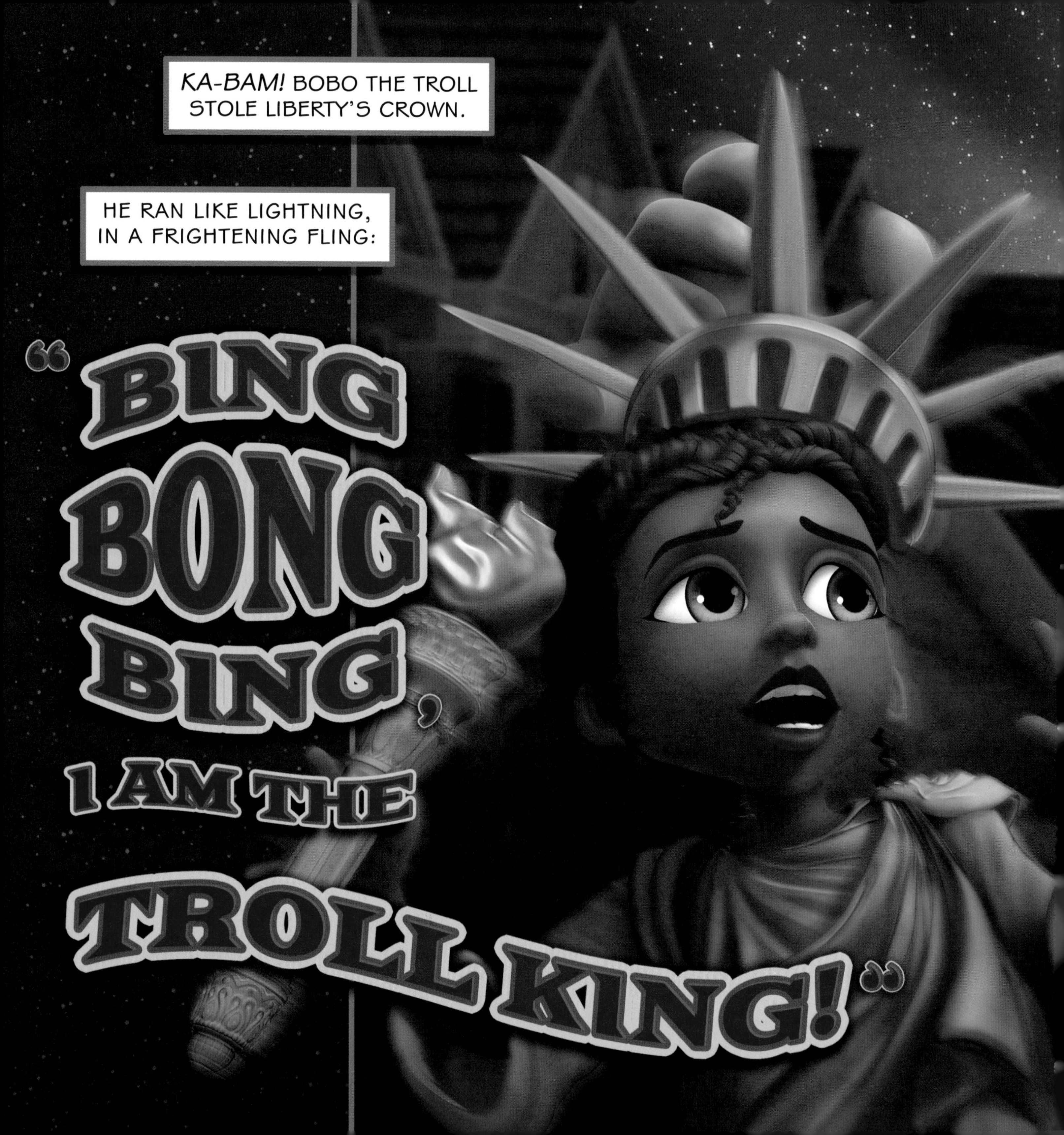
KA-BAM! BOBO THE TROLL STOLE LIBERTY'S CROWN.
HE RAN LIKE LIGHTNING, IN A FRIGHTENING FLING:
"BING BONG BING, I AM THE TROLL KING!"

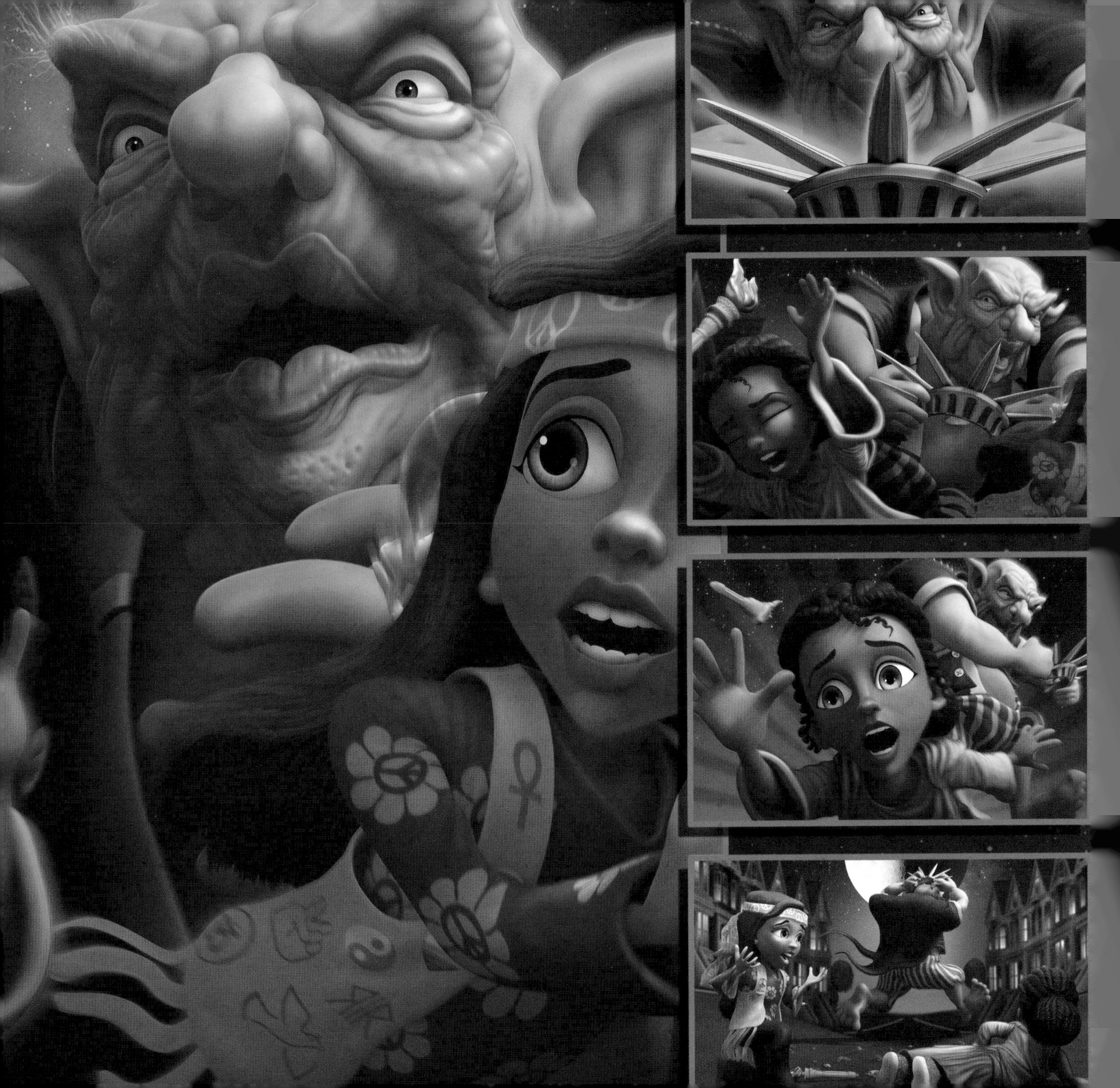

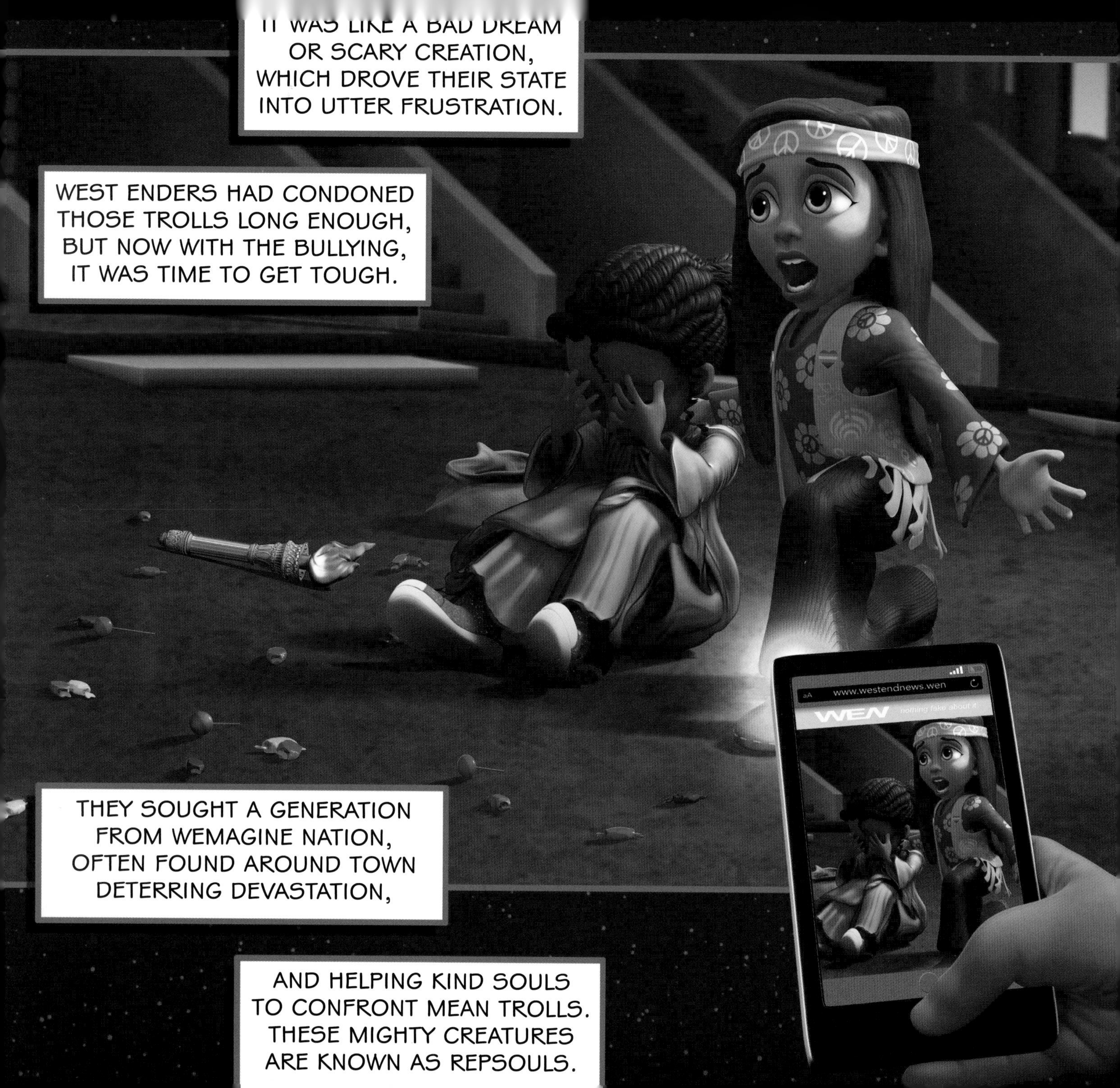
IT WAS LIKE A BAD DREAM
OR SCARY CREATION,
WHICH DROVE THEIR STATE
INTO UTTER FRUSTRATION.
WEST ENDERS HAD CONDONED
THOSE TROLLS LONG ENOUGH,
BUT NOW WITH THE BULLYING,
IT WAS TIME TO GET TOUGH.
www.westendnews.wen
WEN
nothing fake about it
THEY SOUGHT A GENERATION
FROM WEMAGINE NATION,
OFTEN FOUND AROUND TOWN
DETERRING DEVASTATION,
AND HELPING KIND SOULS
TO CONFRONT MEAN TROLLS.
THESE MIGHTY CREATURES
ARE KNOWN AS REPSOULS.

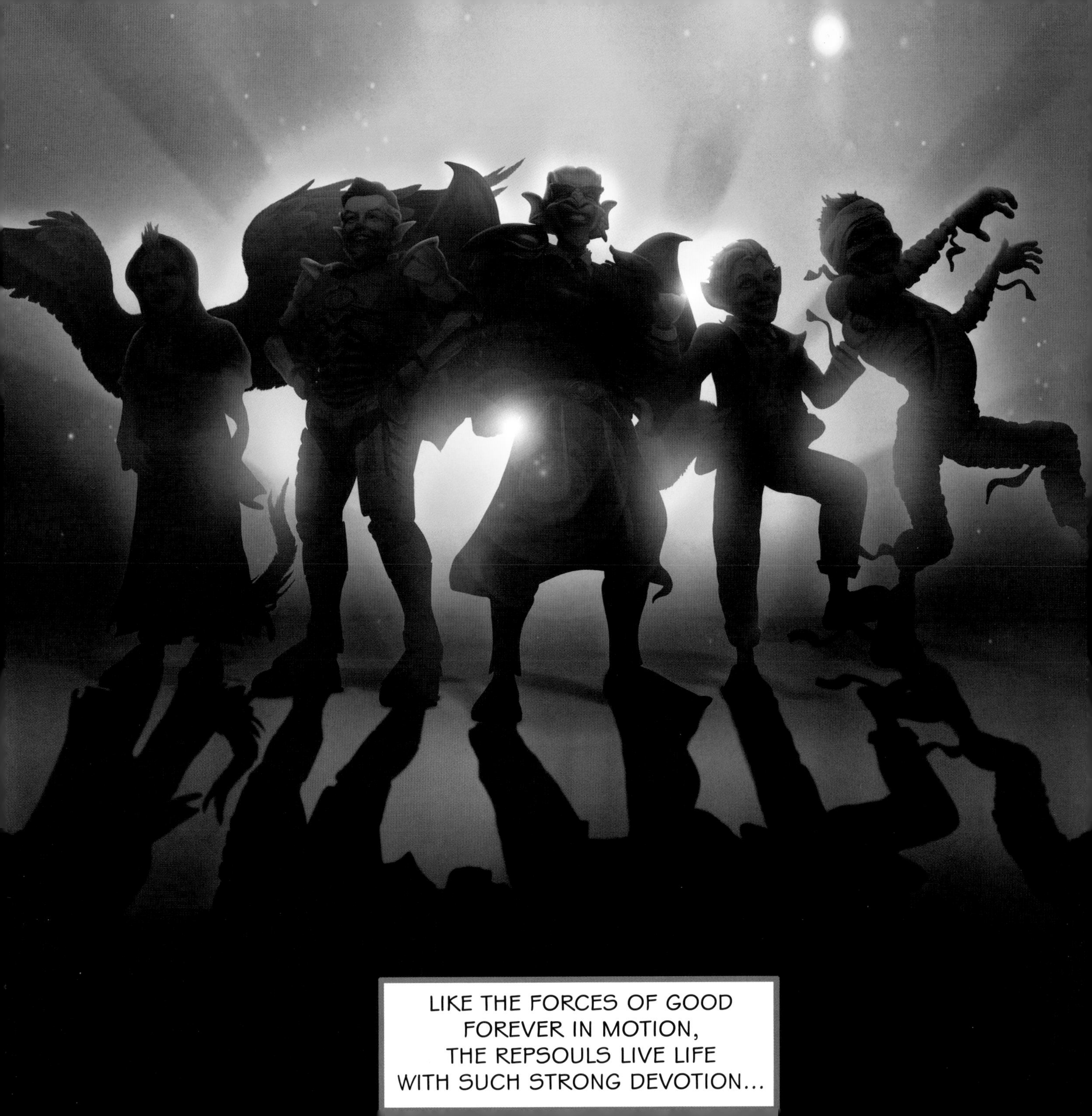
LIKE THE FORCES OF GOOD
FOREVER IN MOTION,
THE REPSOULS LIVE LIFE
WITH SUCH STRONG DEVOTION...

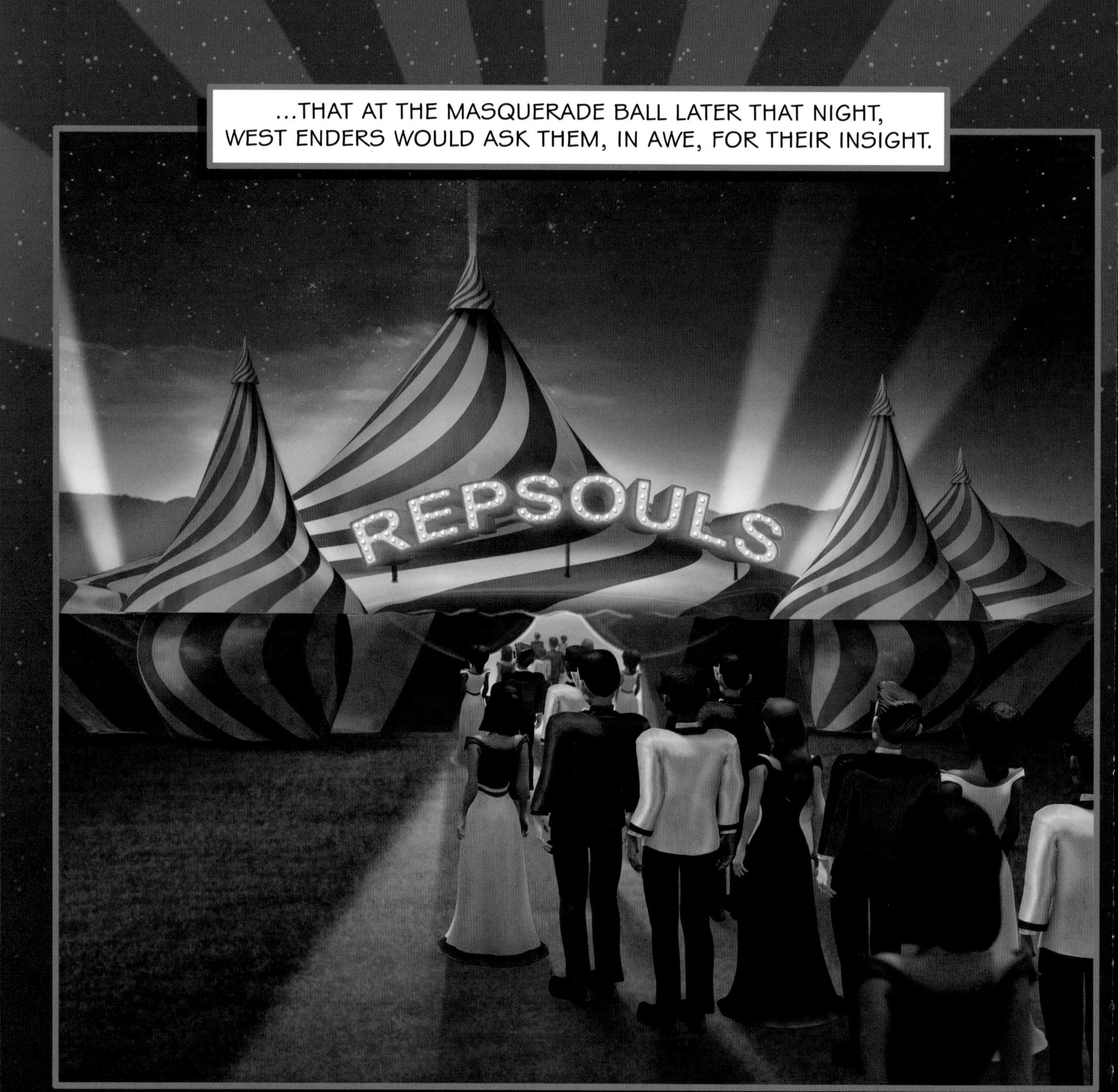
...THAT AT THE MASQUERADE BALL LATER THAT NIGHT, WEST ENDERS WOULD ASK THEM, IN AWE, FOR THEIR INSIGHT.
REPSOULS

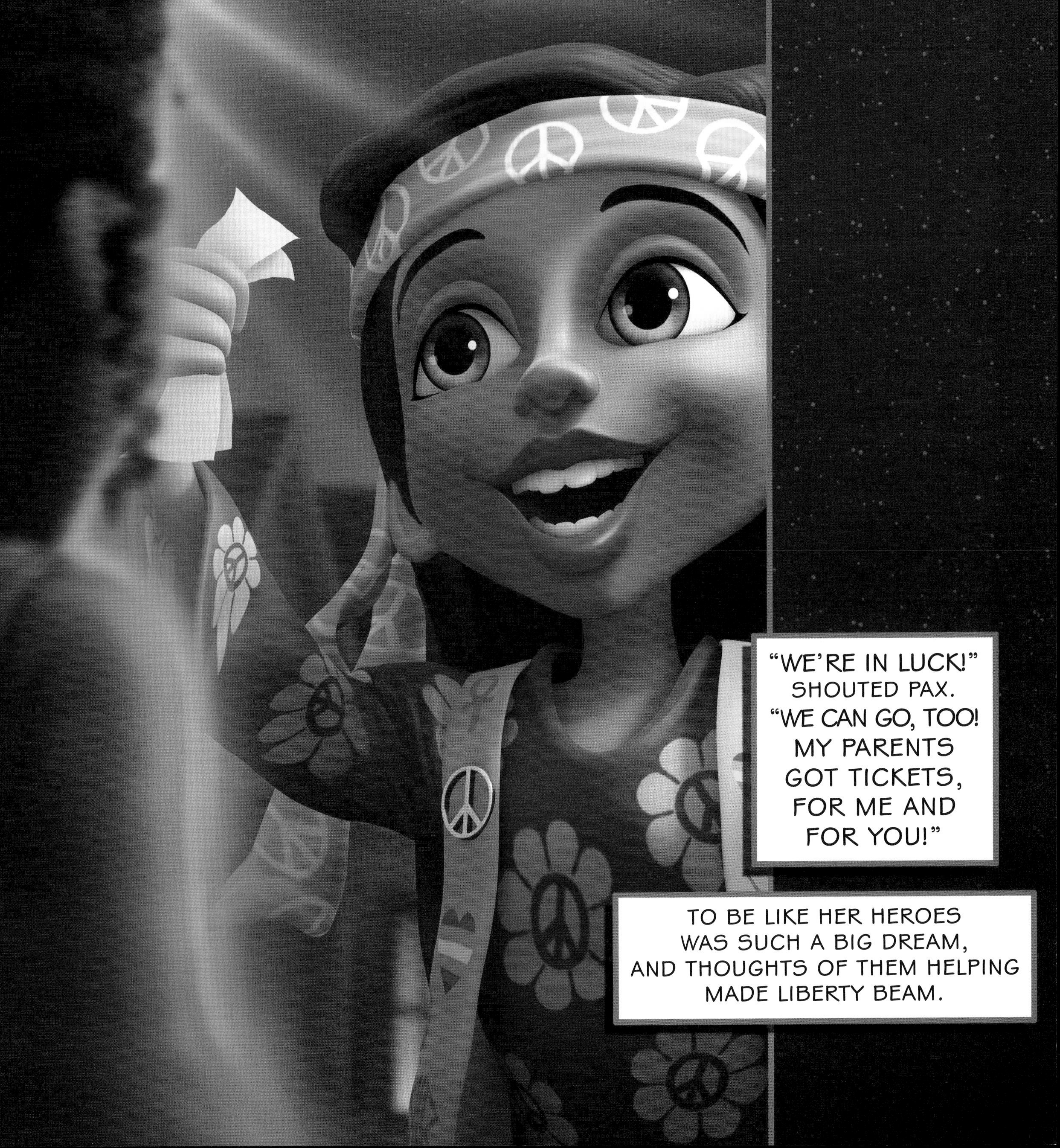
"WE'RE IN LUCK!" SHOUTED PAX. "WE CAN GO, TOO! MY PARENTS GOT TICKETS, FOR ME AND FOR YOU!"
TO BE LIKE HER HEROES WAS SUCH A BIG DREAM, AND THOUGHTS OF THEM HELPING MADE LIBERTY BEAM.

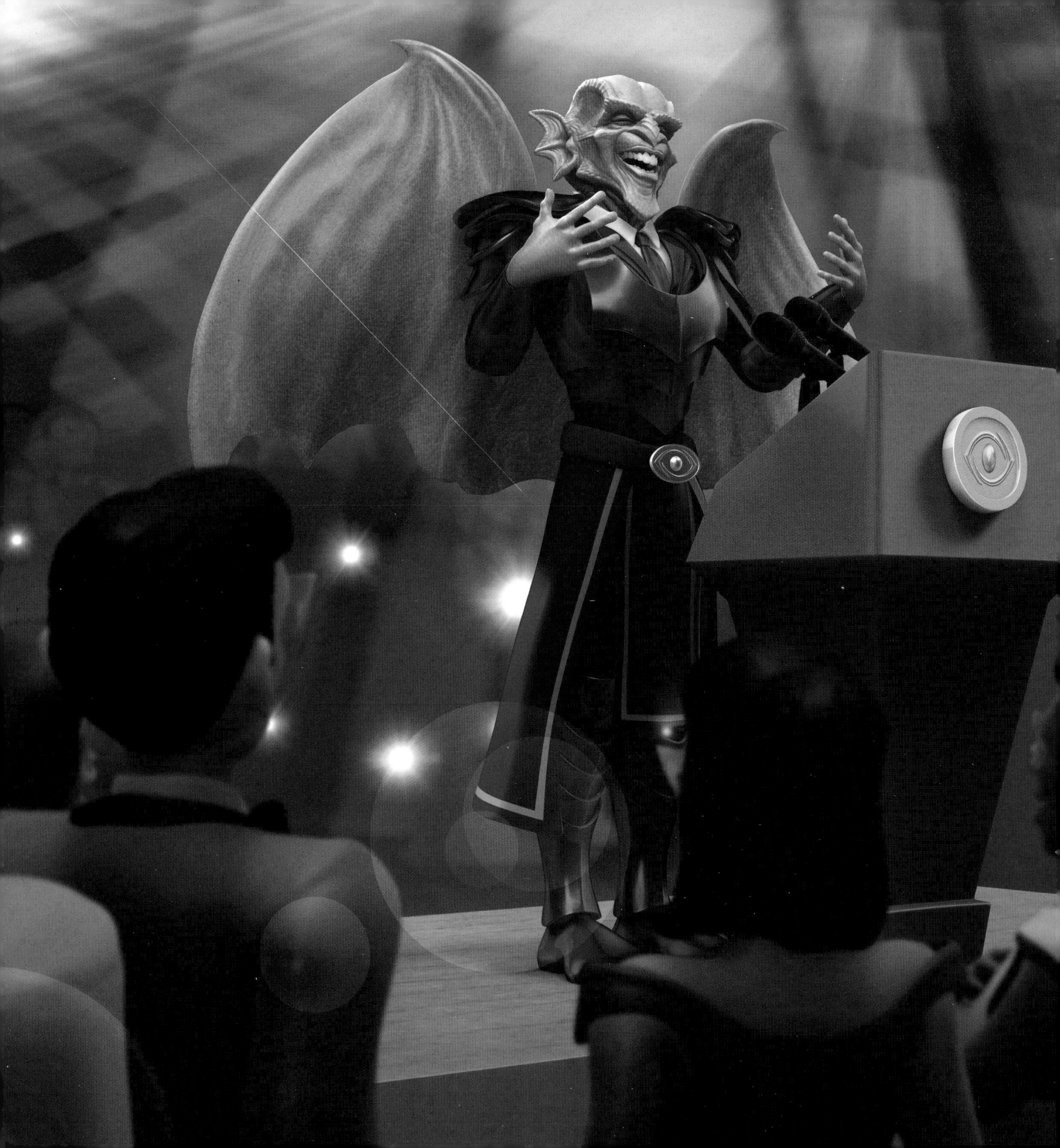

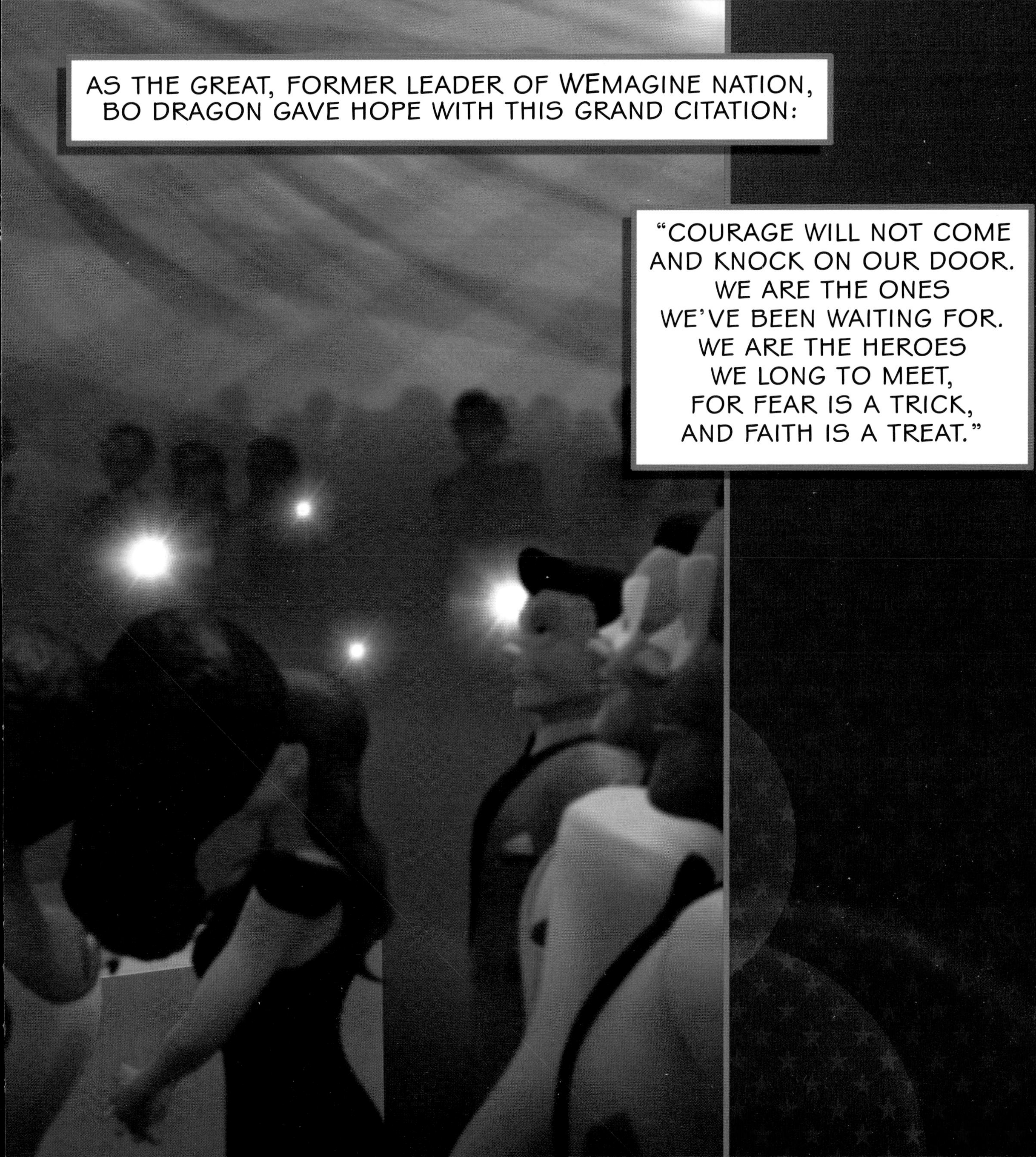
AS THE GREAT, FORMER LEADER OF WEMAGINE NATION, BO DRAGON GAVE HOPE WITH THIS GRAND CITATION:
"COURAGE WILL NOT COME AND KNOCK ON OUR DOOR. WE ARE THE ONES WE'VE BEEN WAITING FOR. WE ARE THE HEROES WE LONG TO MEET, FOR FEAR IS A TRICK, AND FAITH IS A TREAT."

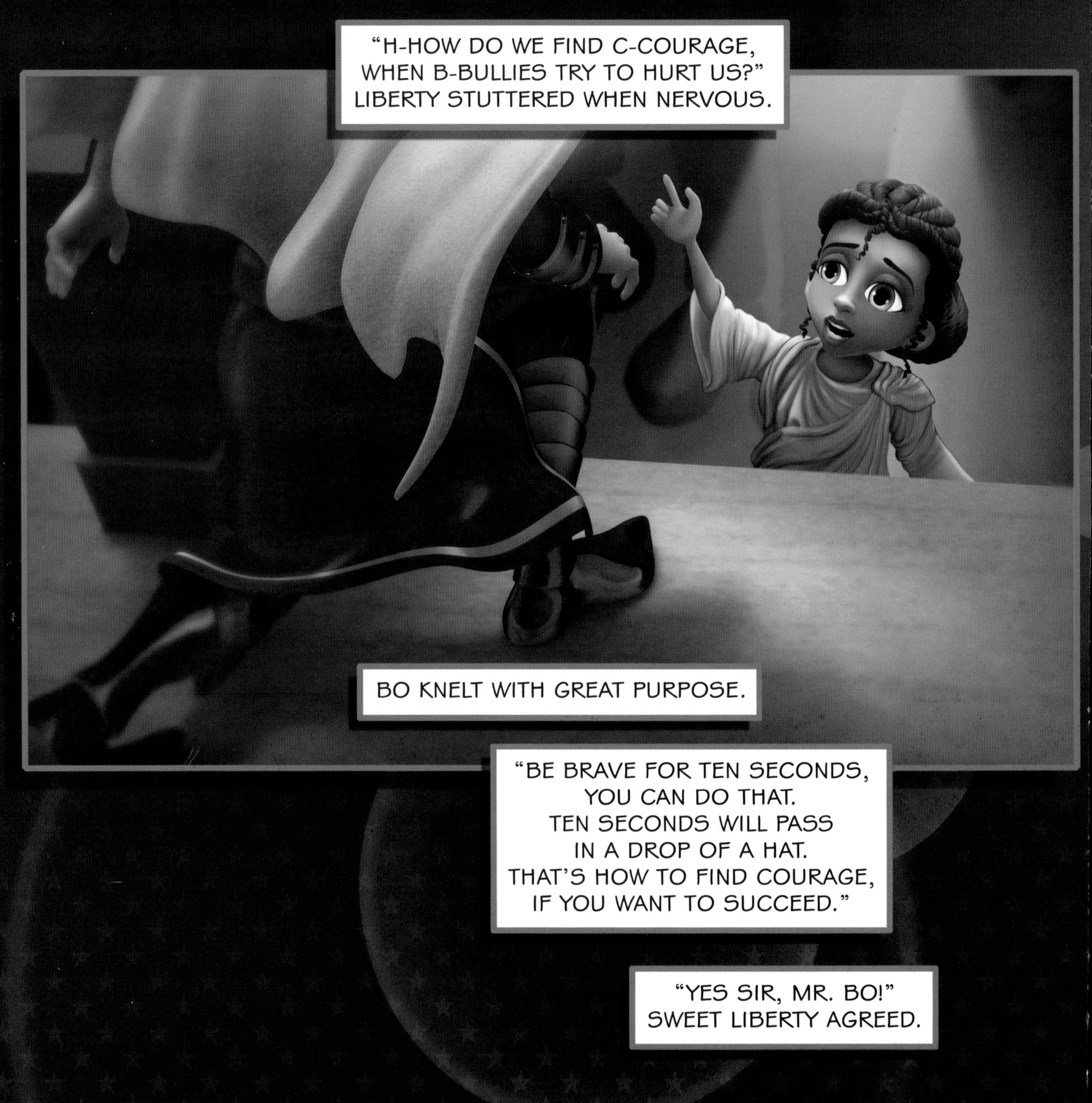
"H-HOW DO WE FIND C-COURAGE, WHEN B-BULLIES TRY TO HURT US?" LIBERTY STUTTERED WHEN NERVOUS.
BO KNELT WITH GREAT PURPOSE.
"BE BRAVE FOR TEN SECONDS, YOU CAN DO THAT. TEN SECONDS WILL PASS IN A DROP OF A HAT. THAT'S HOW TO FIND COURAGE, IF YOU WANT TO SUCCEED."
"YES SIR, MR. BO!" SWEET LIBERTY AGREED.

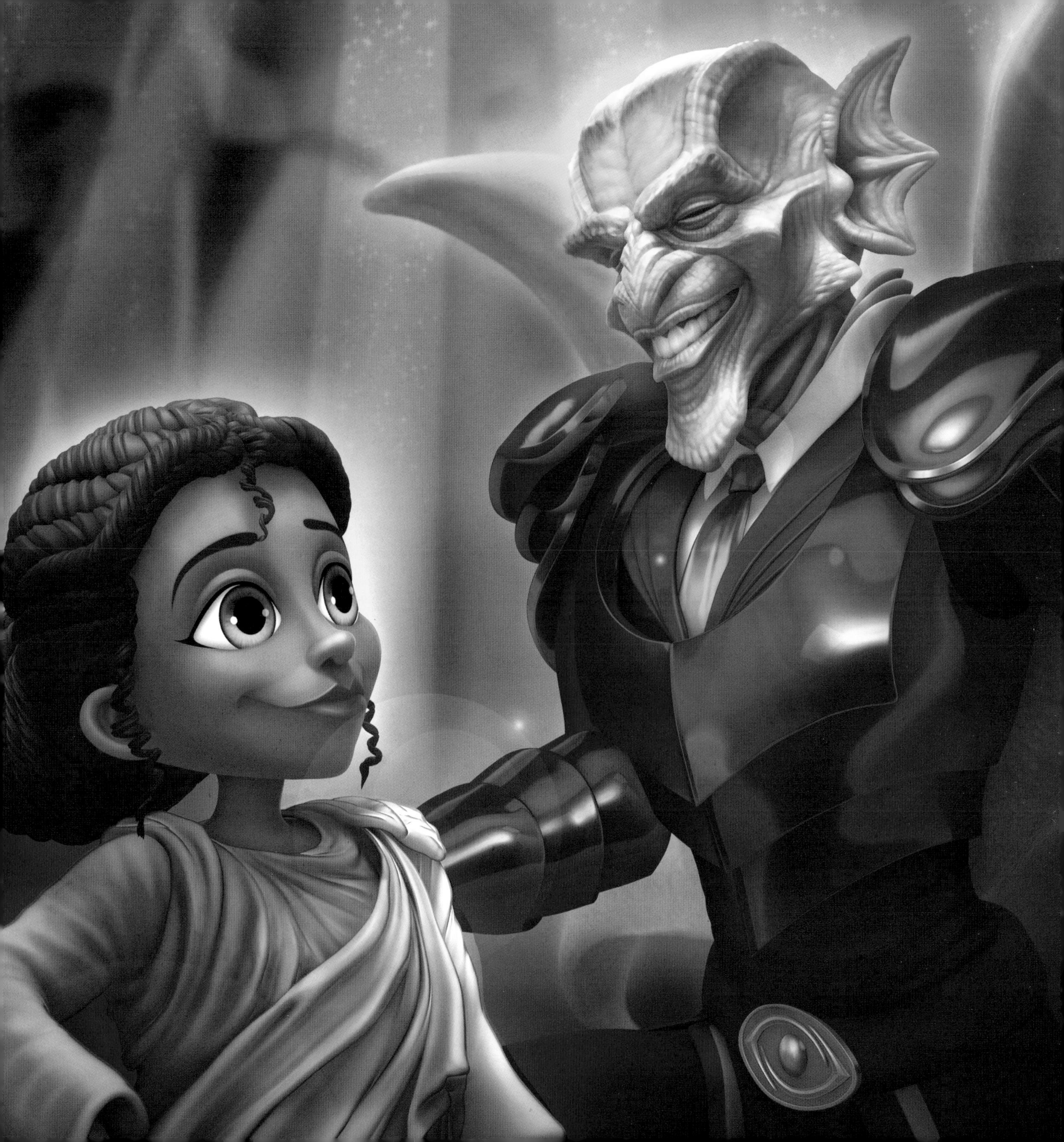

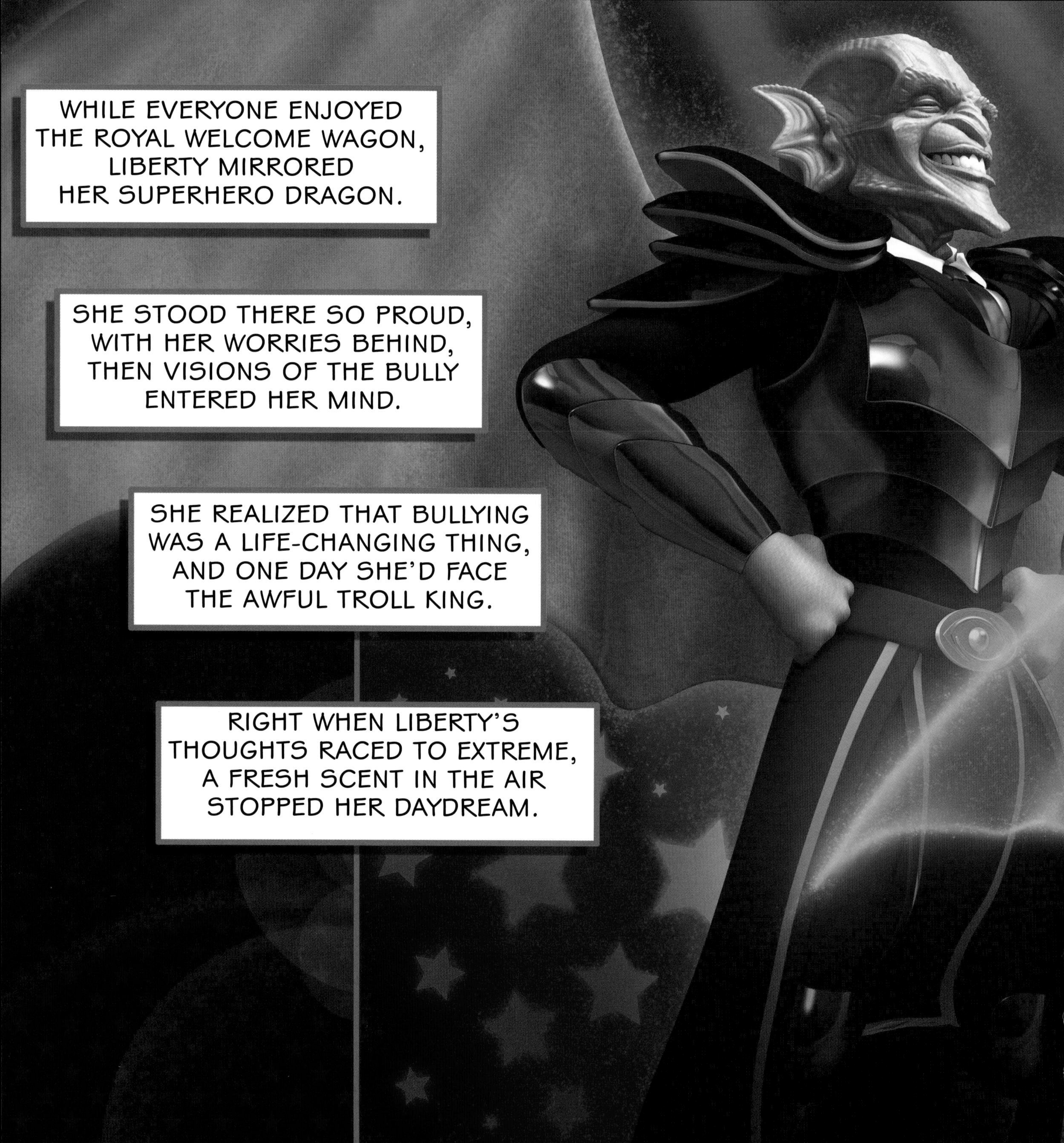
WHILE EVERYONE ENJOYED THE ROYAL WELCOME WAGON, LIBERTY MIRRORED HER SUPERHERO DRAGON.
SHE STOOD THERE SO PROUD, WITH HER WORRIES BEHIND, THEN VISIONS OF THE BULLY ENTERED HER MIND.
SHE REALIZED THAT BULLYING WAS A LIFE-CHANGING THING, AND ONE DAY SHE'D FACE THE AWFUL TROLL KING.
RIGHT WHEN LIBERTY'S THOUGHTS RACED TO EXTREME, A FRESH SCENT IN THE AIR STOPPED HER DAYDREAM.

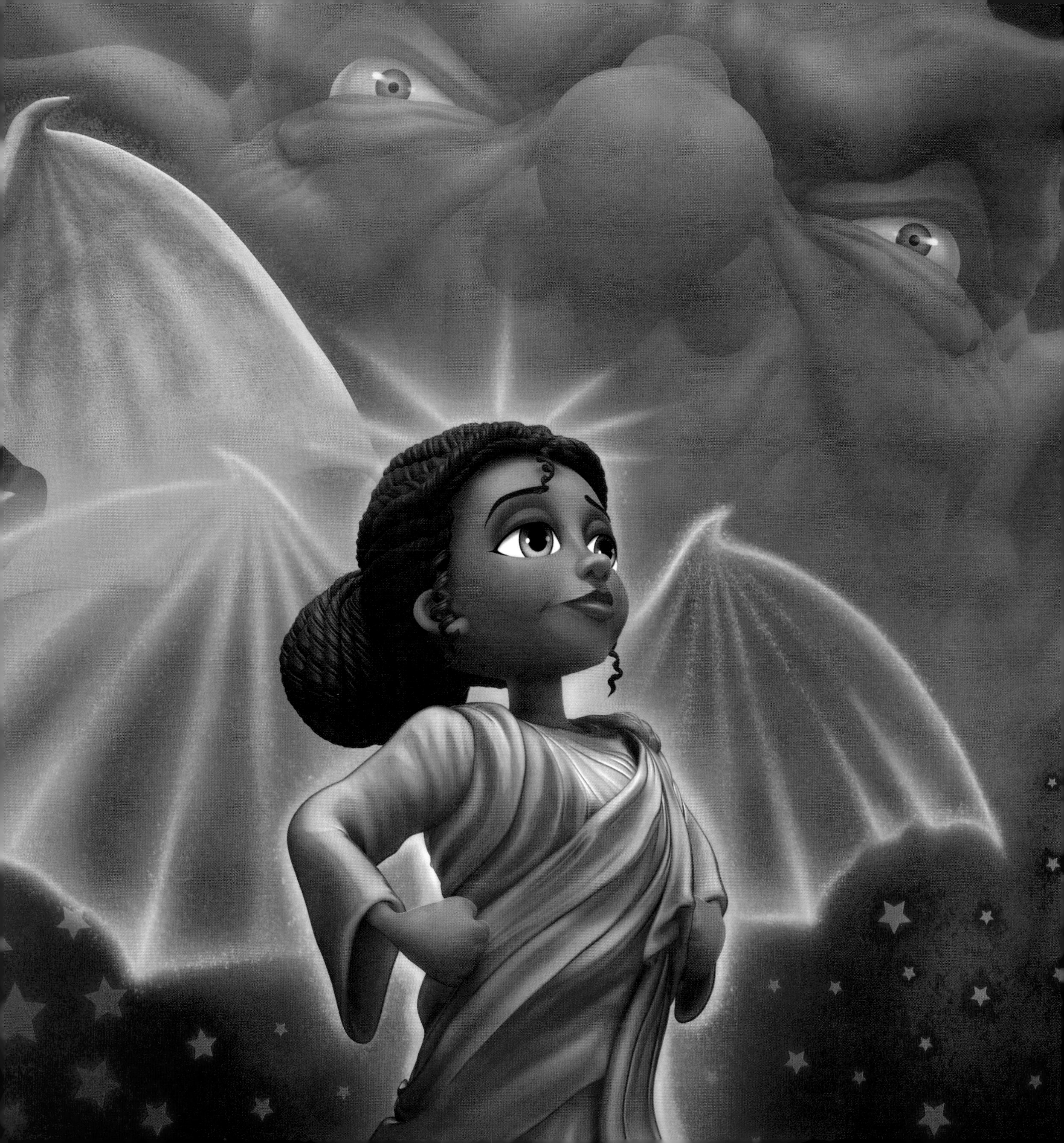

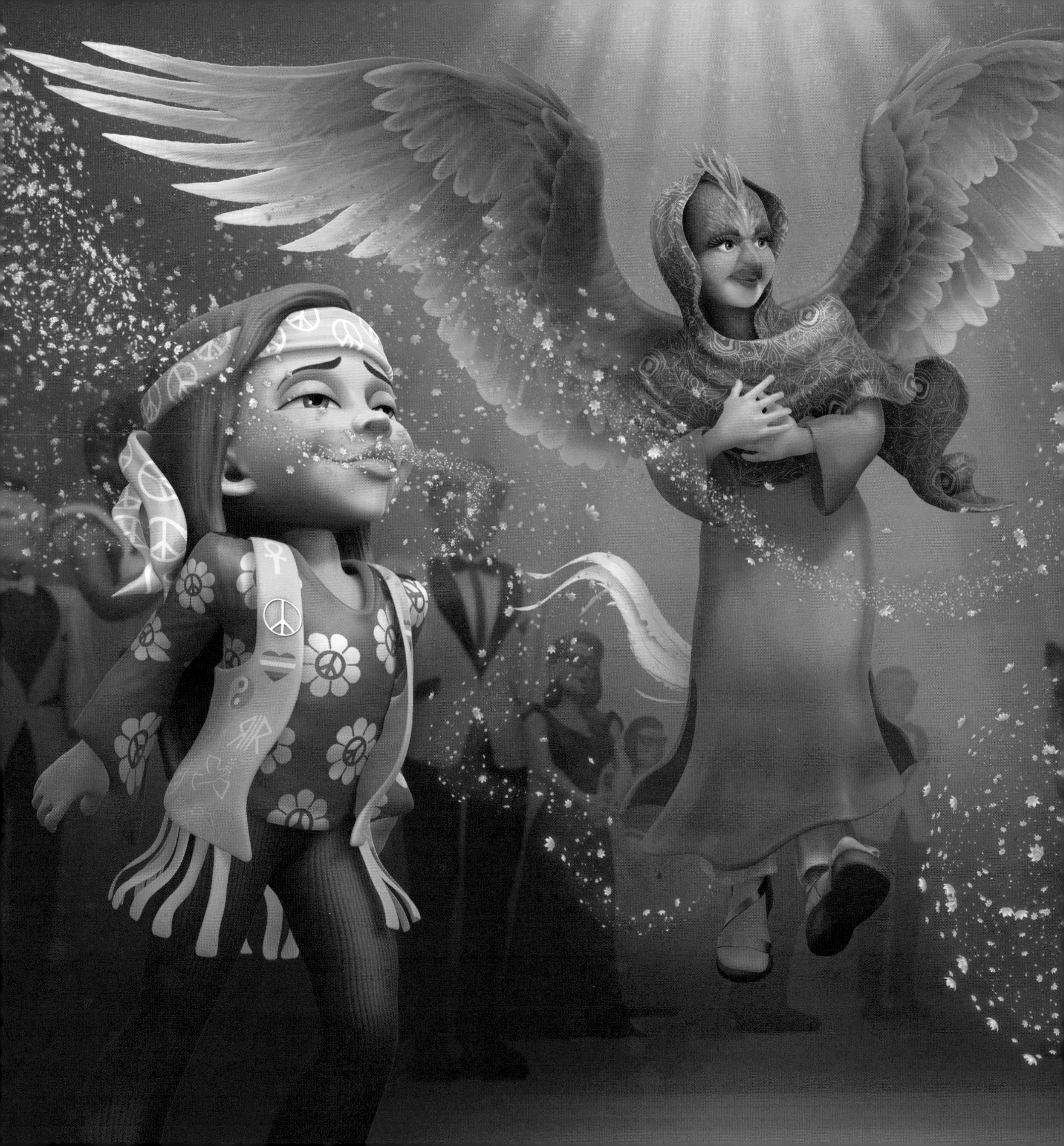

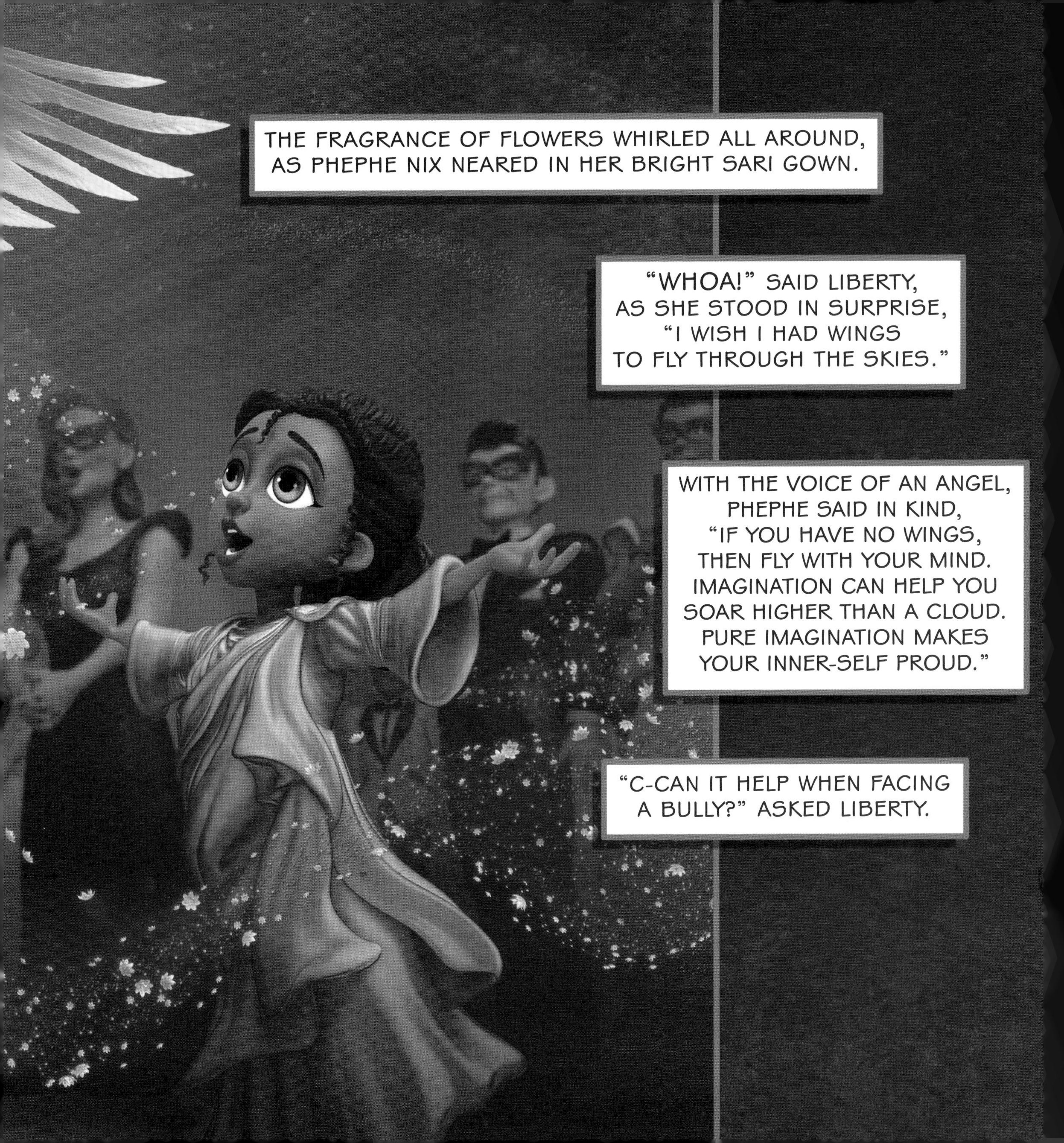
THE FRAGRANCE OF FLOWERS WHIRLED ALL AROUND, AS PHEPHE NIX NEARED IN HER BRIGHT SARI GOWN.
"WHOA!" SAID LIBERTY, AS SHE STOOD IN SURPRISE, "I WISH I HAD WINGS TO FLY THROUGH THE SKIES."
WITH THE VOICE OF AN ANGEL, PHEPHE SAID IN KIND, "IF YOU HAVE NO WINGS, THEN FLY WITH YOUR MIND. IMAGINATION CAN HELP YOU SOAR HIGHER THAN A CLOUD. PURE IMAGINATION MAKES YOUR INNER-SELF PROUD."
"C-CAN IT HELP WHEN FACING A BULLY?" ASKED LIBERTY.

IN TURN, PHEPHE ANSWERED
WITH SUCH CERTAINTY:
"INDEED, CREATIVE THINKING
SPAWNED EVERY GREAT THING,
FROM FLYING MACHINES
TO CROWNING A QUEEN,
AND BEST OF ALL,
A BULLY VACCINE."

"WHAT THE HECK DO YOU MEAN
BY A BULLY VACCINE?"

WITH MAGICAL FLOWERS,
PHEPHE CONJURED A SCENE:
"WE'LL ALWAYS HAVE BULLIES,
THEY GET SMARTER EVERY DAY,
SO, WE MUST BE CREATIVE
TO KEEP THEM AT BAY.

THE FOUNDATION
FOR A BULLY VACCINATION
IS OUR OWN COURAGE
AND VAST IMAGINATION.
ADD AN EDUCATION
AND THERE'S NO LIMITATION
ON HOW HIGH WE FLY
OUR POWERFUL CREATION."

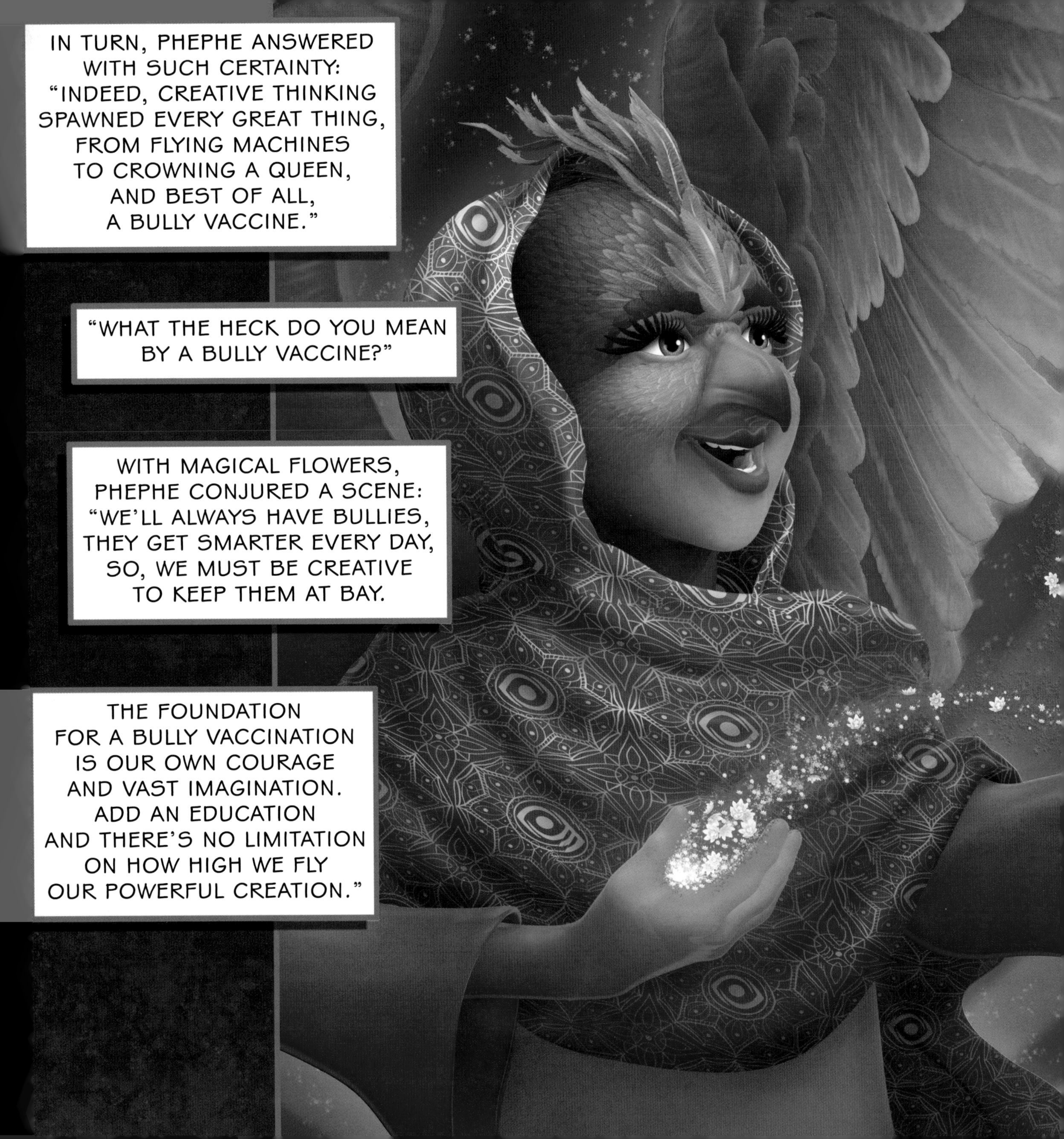

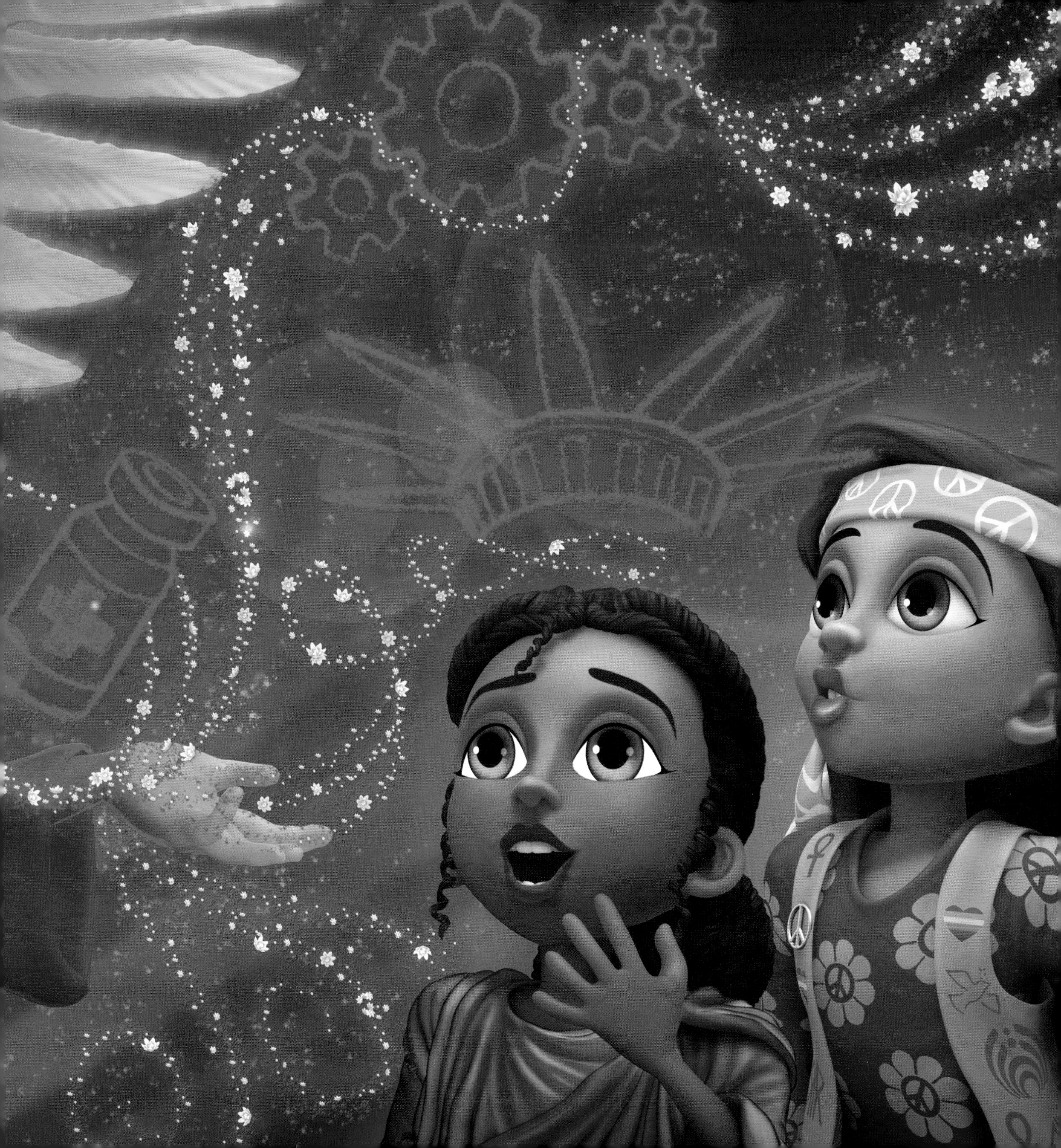

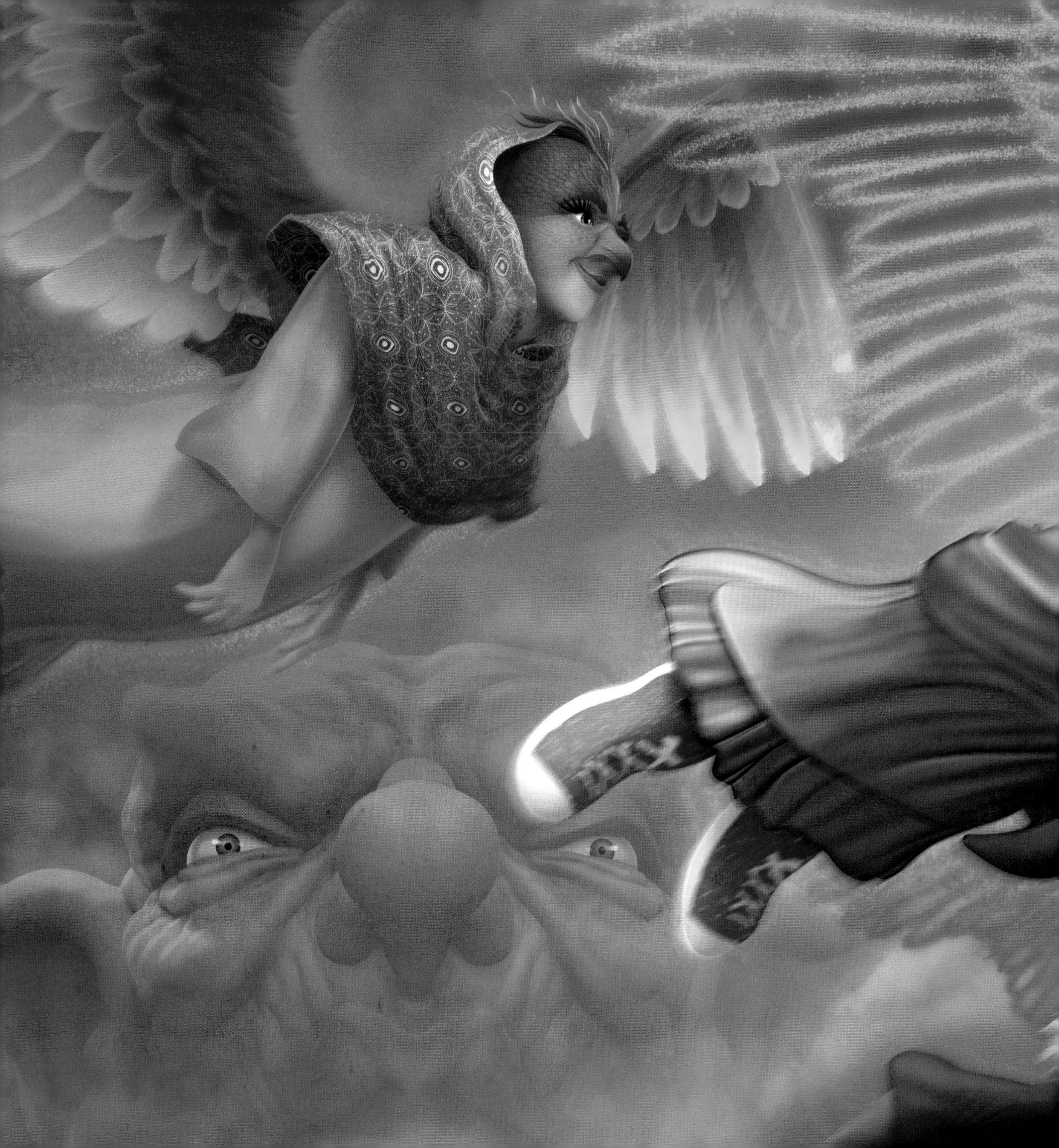

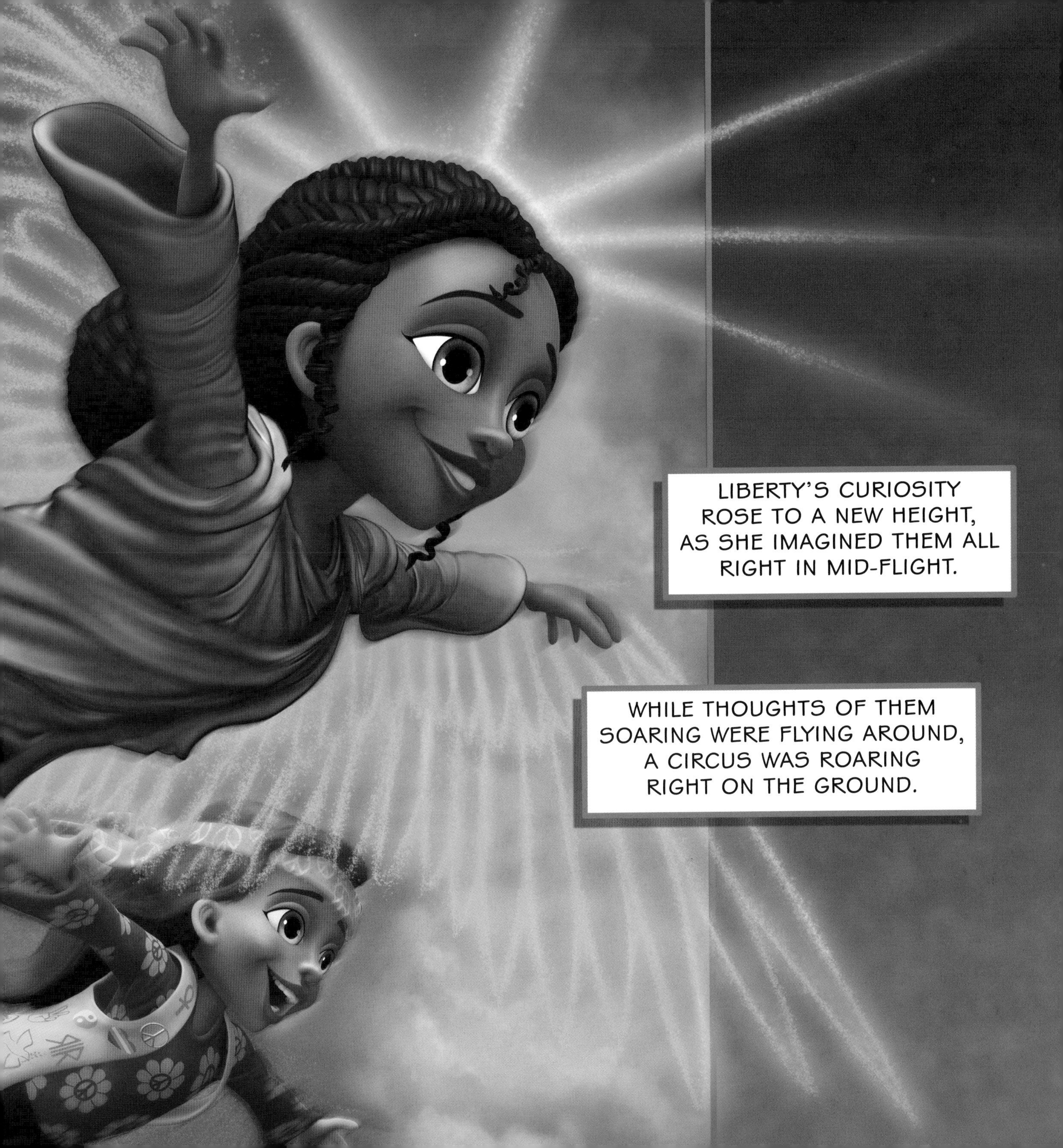

LIBERTY'S CURIOSITY
ROSE TO A NEW HEIGHT,
AS SHE IMAGINED THEM ALL
RIGHT IN MID-FLIGHT.

WHILE THOUGHTS OF THEM
SOARING WERE FLYING AROUND,
A CIRCUS WAS ROARING
RIGHT ON THE GROUND.

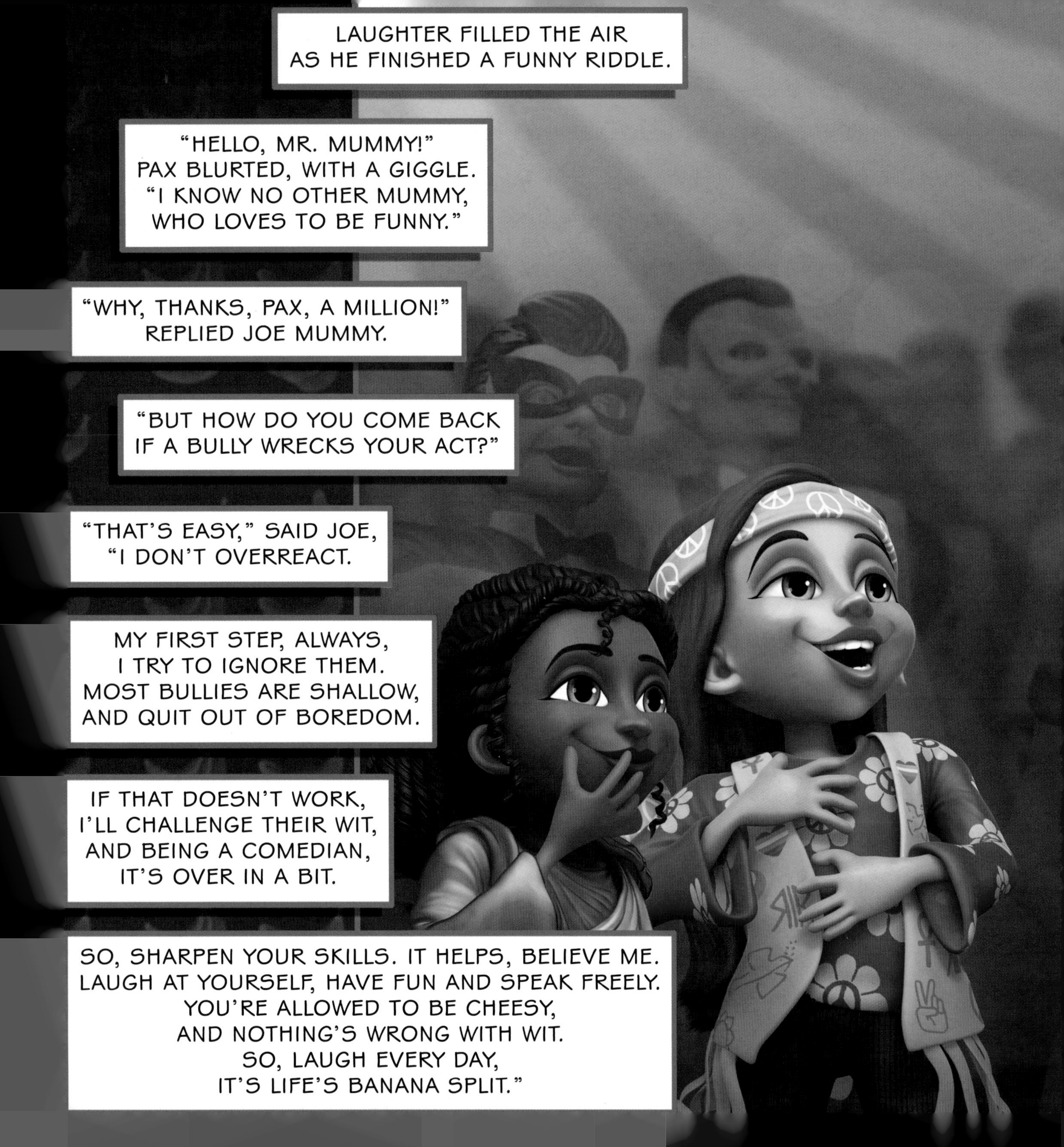
LAUGHTER FILLED THE AIR
AS HE FINISHED A FUNNY RIDDLE.
"HELLO, MR. MUMMY!"
PAX BLURTED, WITH A GIGGLE.
"I KNOW NO OTHER MUMMY,
WHO LOVES TO BE FUNNY."
"WHY, THANKS, PAX, A MILLION!"
REPLIED JOE MUMMY.
"BUT HOW DO YOU COME BACK
IF A BULLY WRECKS YOUR ACT?"
"THAT'S EASY," SAID JOE,
"I DON'T OVERREACT.
MY FIRST STEP, ALWAYS,
I TRY TO IGNORE THEM.
MOST BULLIES ARE SHALLOW,
AND QUIT OUT OF BOREDOM.
IF THAT DOESN'T WORK,
I'LL CHALLENGE THEIR WIT,
AND BEING A COMEDIAN,
IT'S OVER IN A BIT.
SO, SHARPEN YOUR SKILLS. IT HELPS, BELIEVE ME.
LAUGH AT YOURSELF, HAVE FUN AND SPEAK FREELY.
YOU'RE ALLOWED TO BE CHEESY,
AND NOTHING'S WRONG WITH WIT.
SO, LAUGH EVERY DAY,
IT'S LIFE'S BANANA SPLIT."

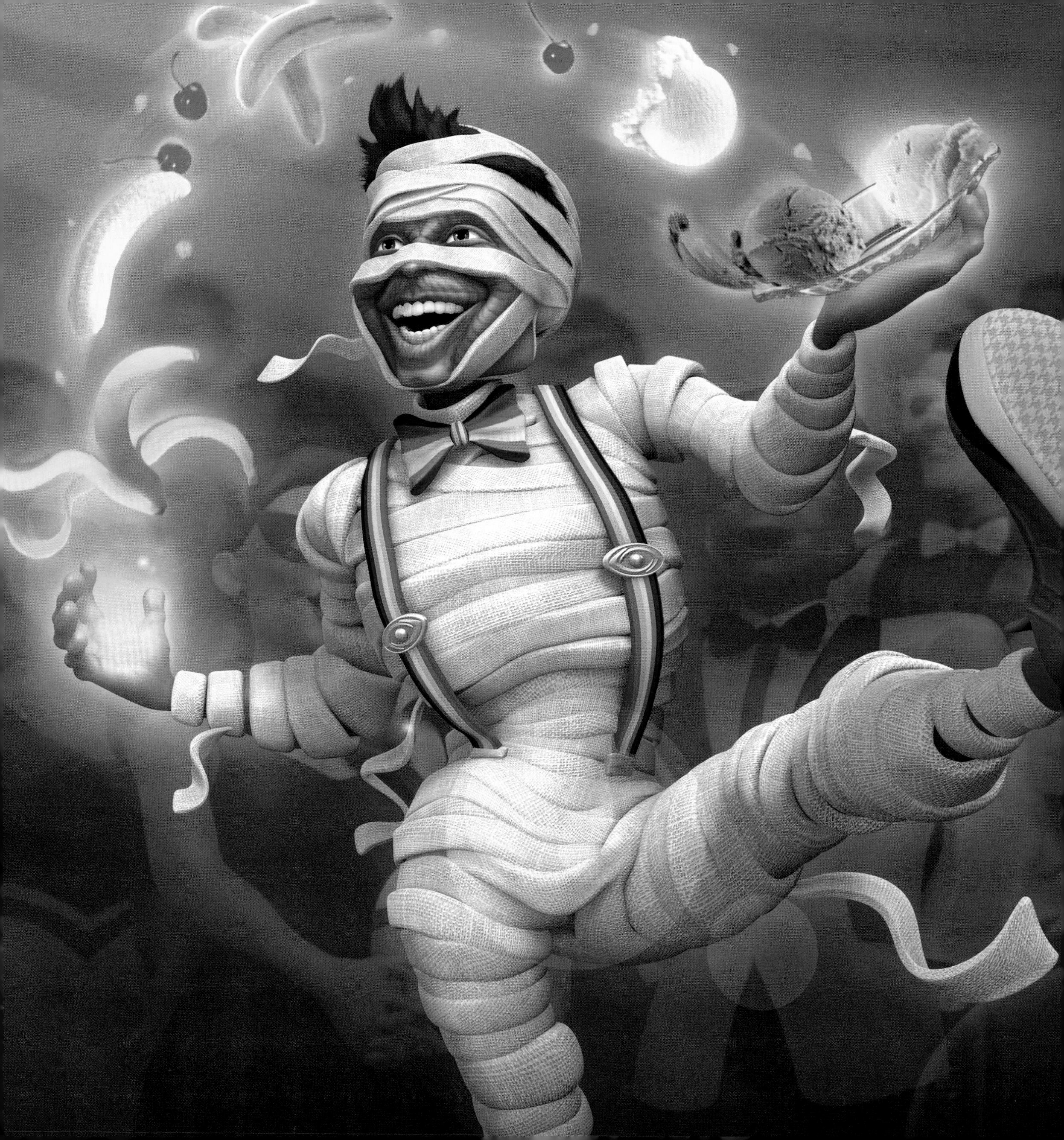

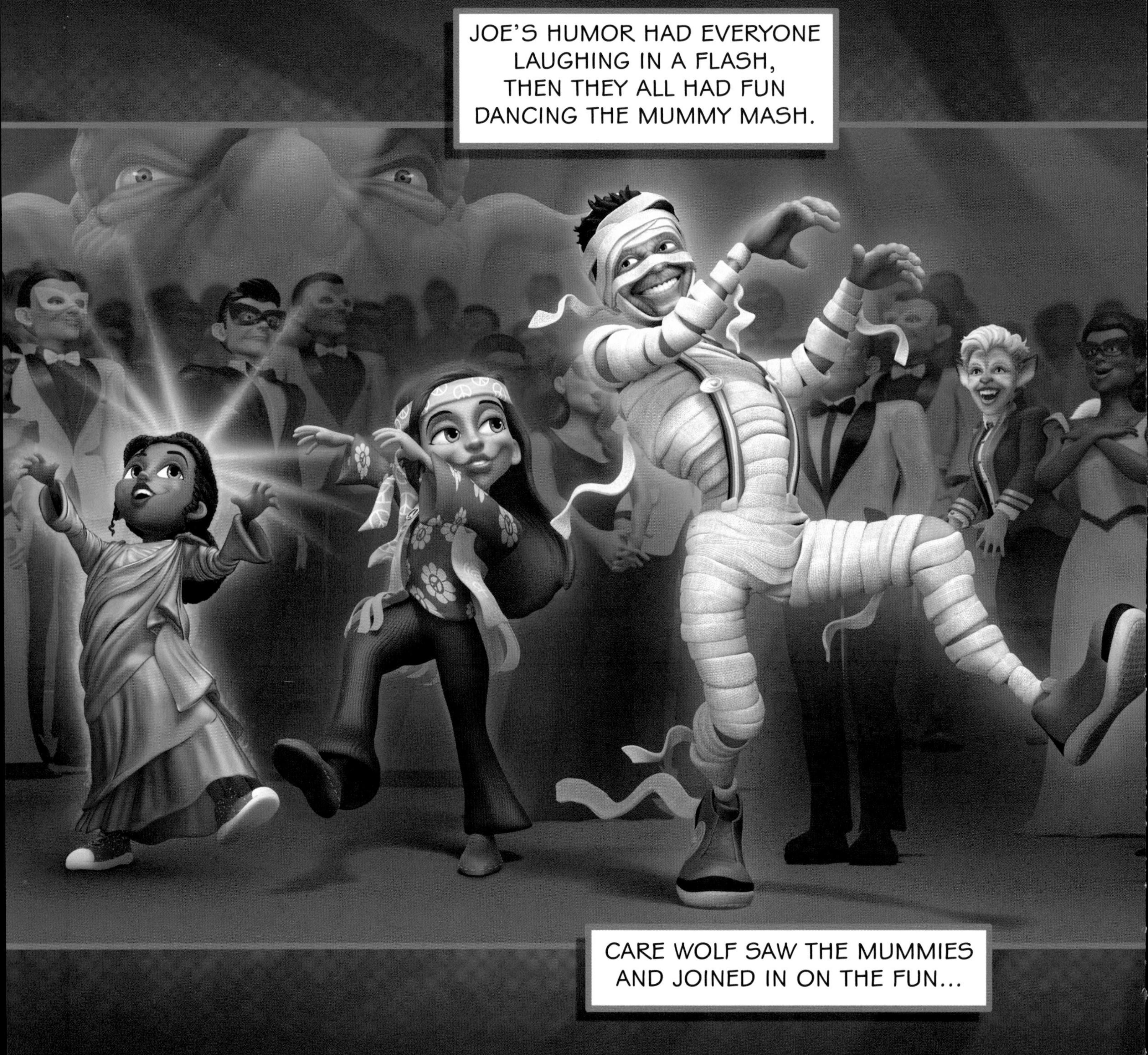
JOE'S HUMOR HAD EVERYONE LAUGHING IN A FLASH, THEN THEY ALL HAD FUN DANCING THE MUMMY MASH.
CARE WOLF SAW THE MUMMIES AND JOINED IN ON THE FUN...

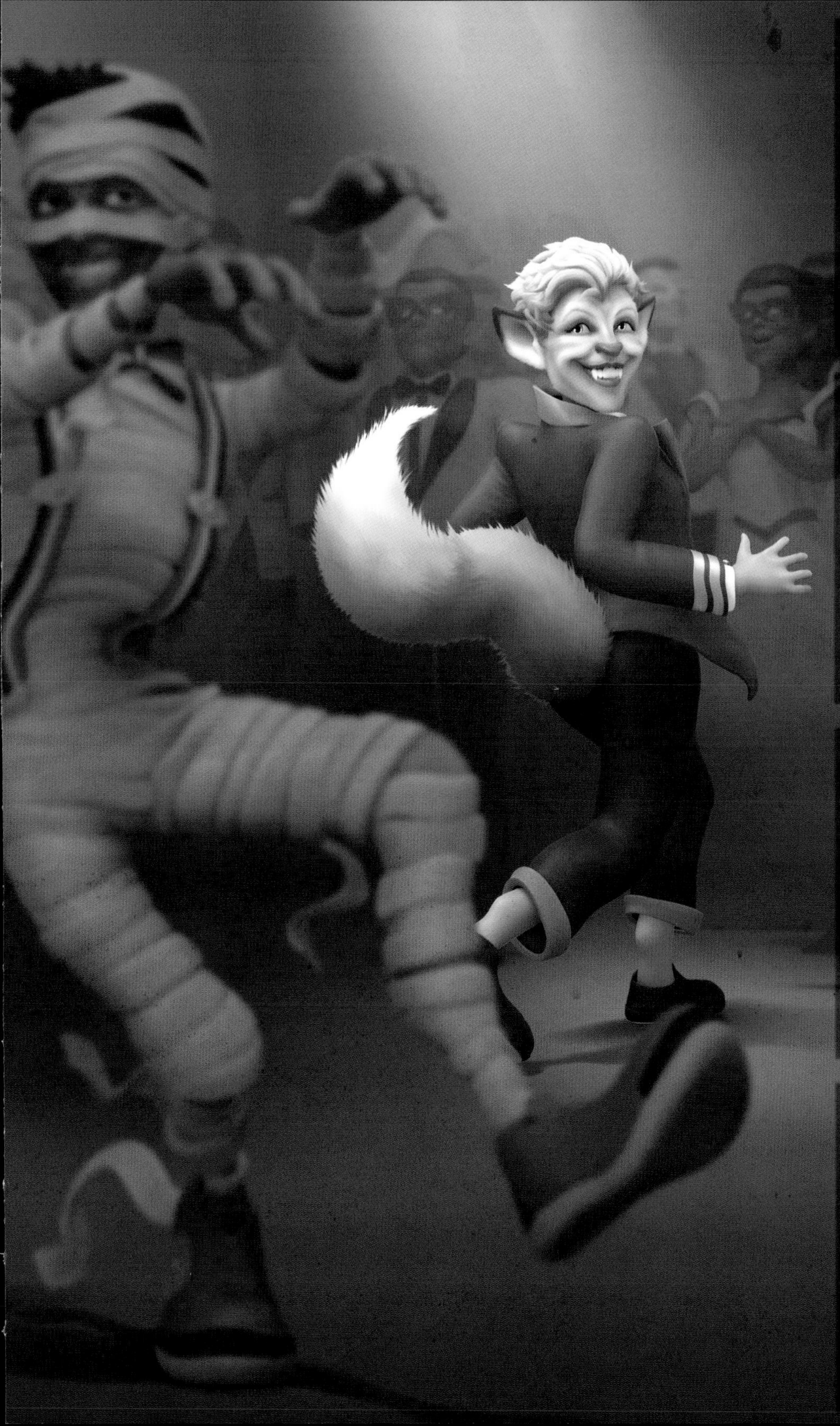
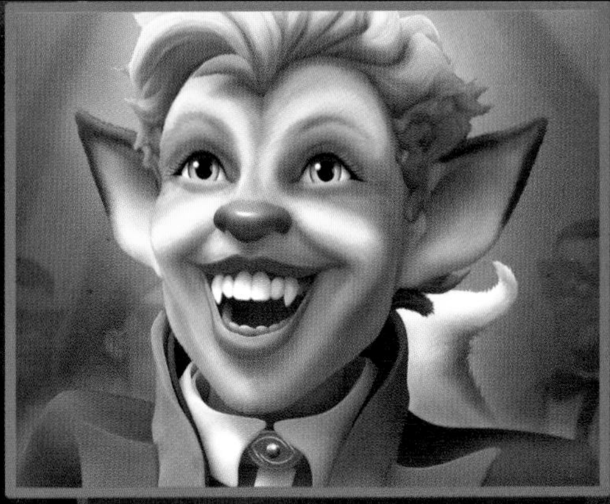
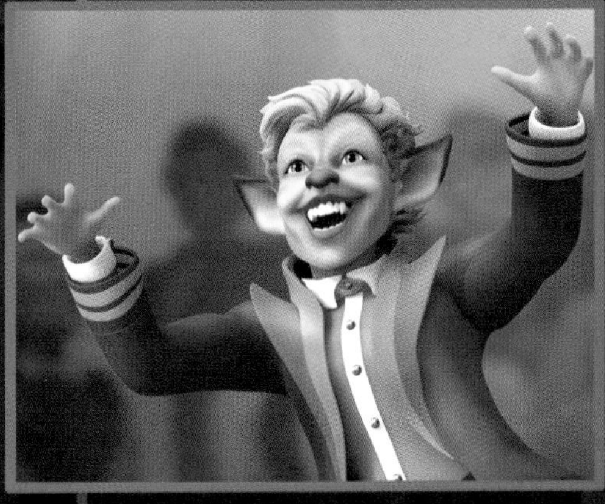
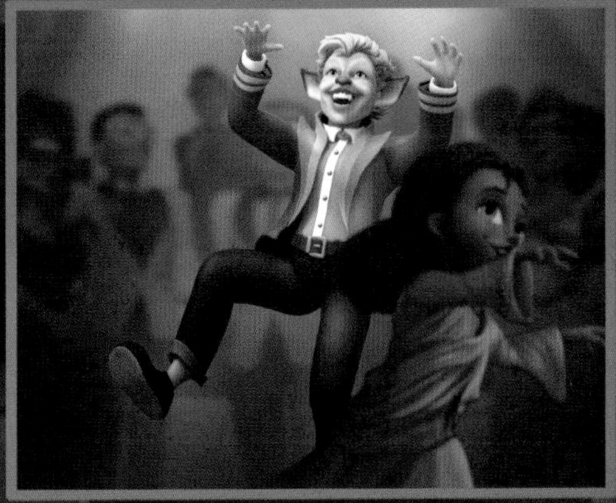
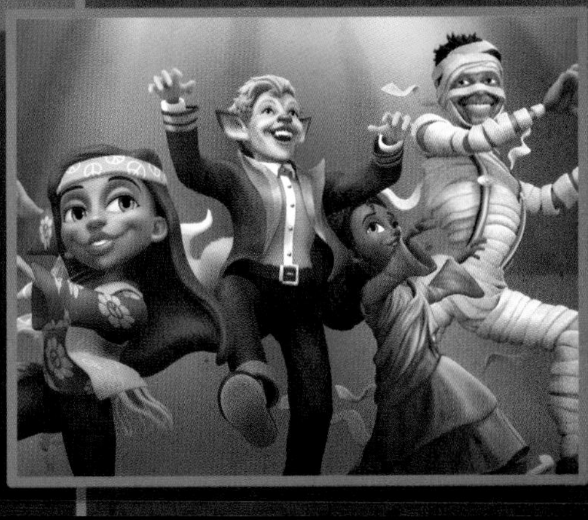

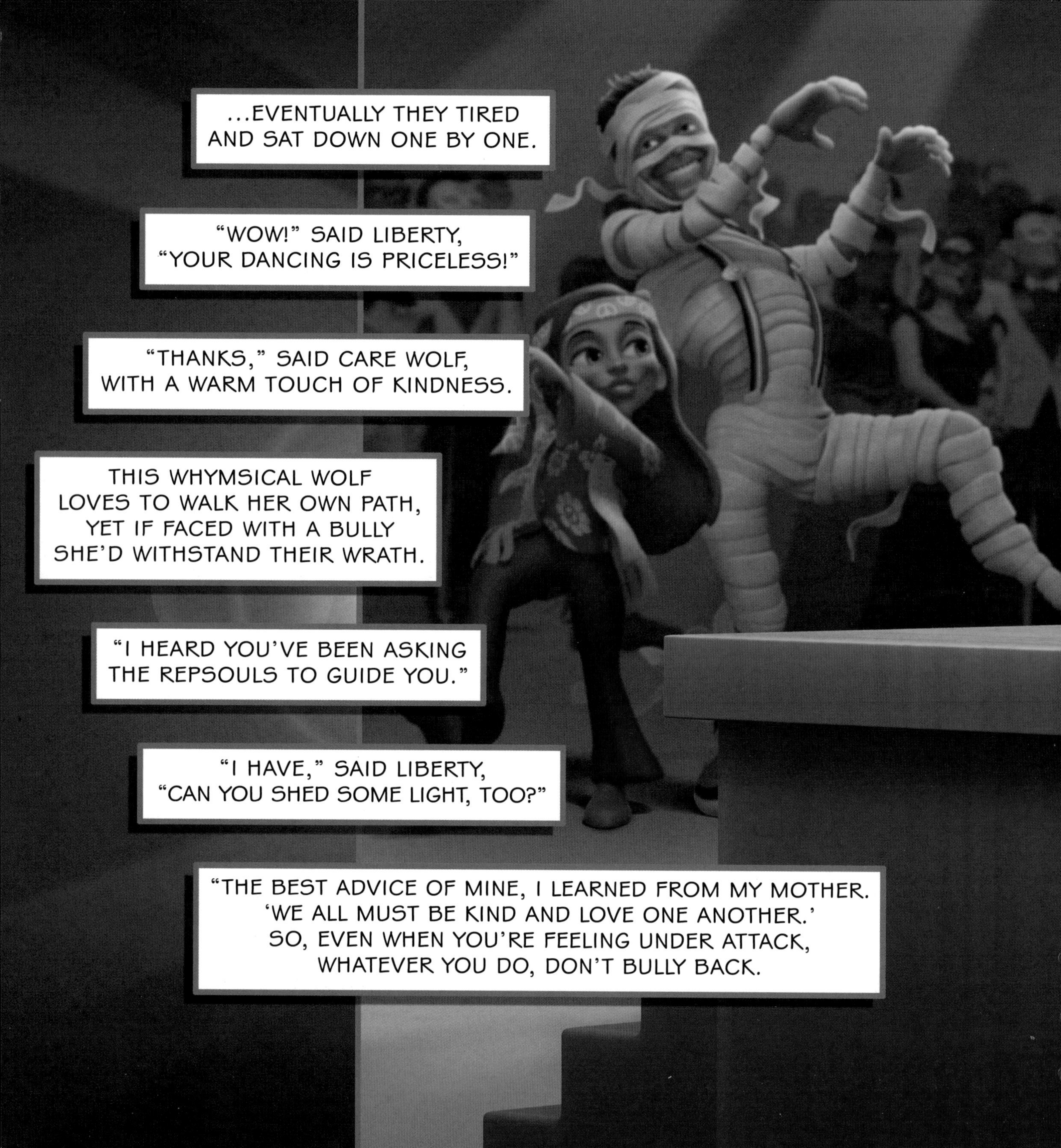
...EVENTUALLY THEY TIRED AND SAT DOWN ONE BY ONE.
"WOW!" SAID LIBERTY, "YOUR DANCING IS PRICELESS!"
"THANKS," SAID CARE WOLF, WITH A WARM TOUCH OF KINDNESS.
THIS WHYMSICAL WOLF LOVES TO WALK HER OWN PATH, YET IF FACED WITH A BULLY SHE'D WITHSTAND THEIR WRATH.
"I HEARD YOU'VE BEEN ASKING THE REPSOULS TO GUIDE YOU."
"I HAVE," SAID LIBERTY, "CAN YOU SHED SOME LIGHT, TOO?"
"THE BEST ADVICE OF MINE, I LEARNED FROM MY MOTHER. 'WE ALL MUST BE KIND AND LOVE ONE ANOTHER.' SO, EVEN WHEN YOU'RE FEELING UNDER ATTACK, WHATEVER YOU DO, DON'T BULLY BACK.

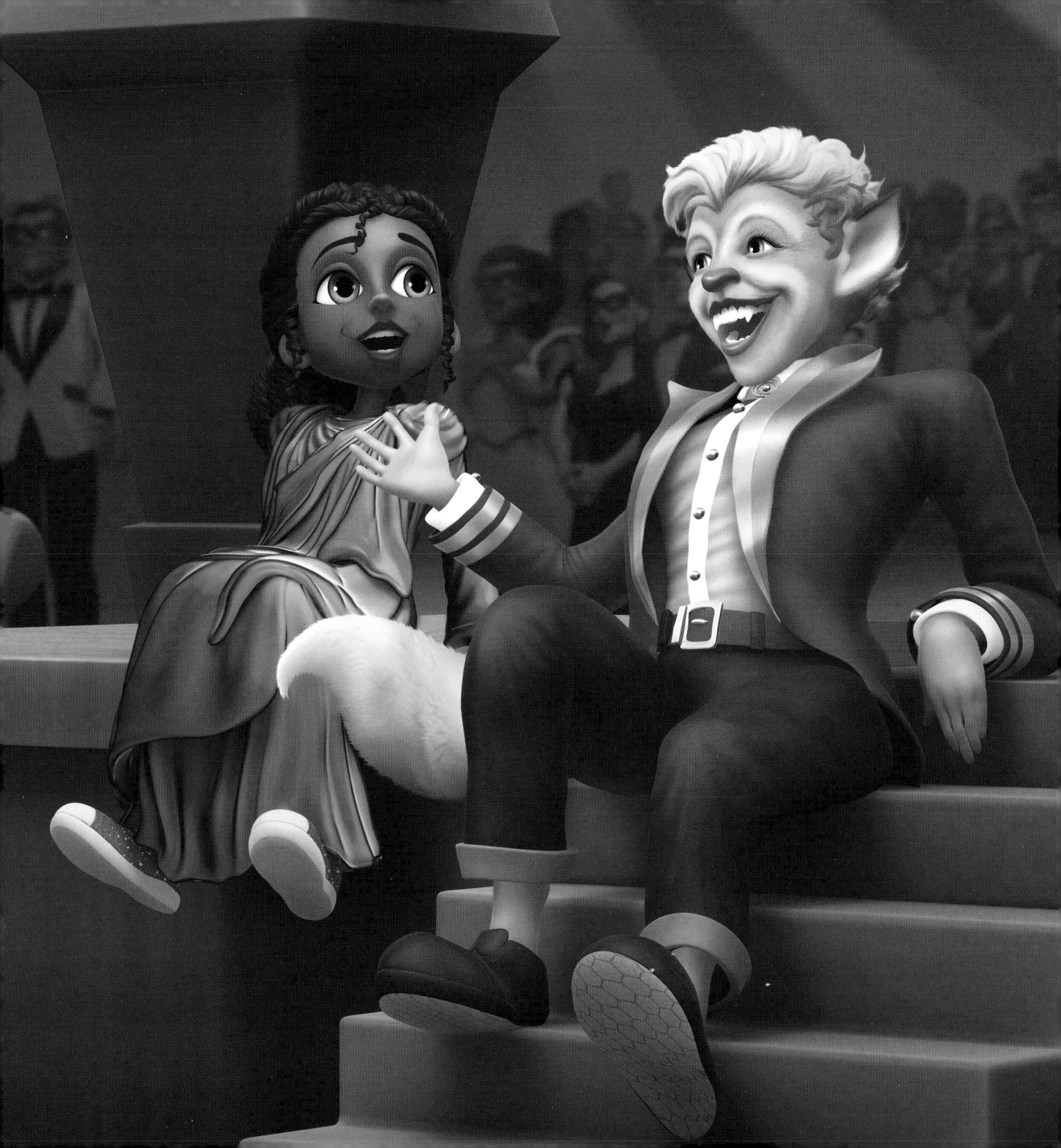

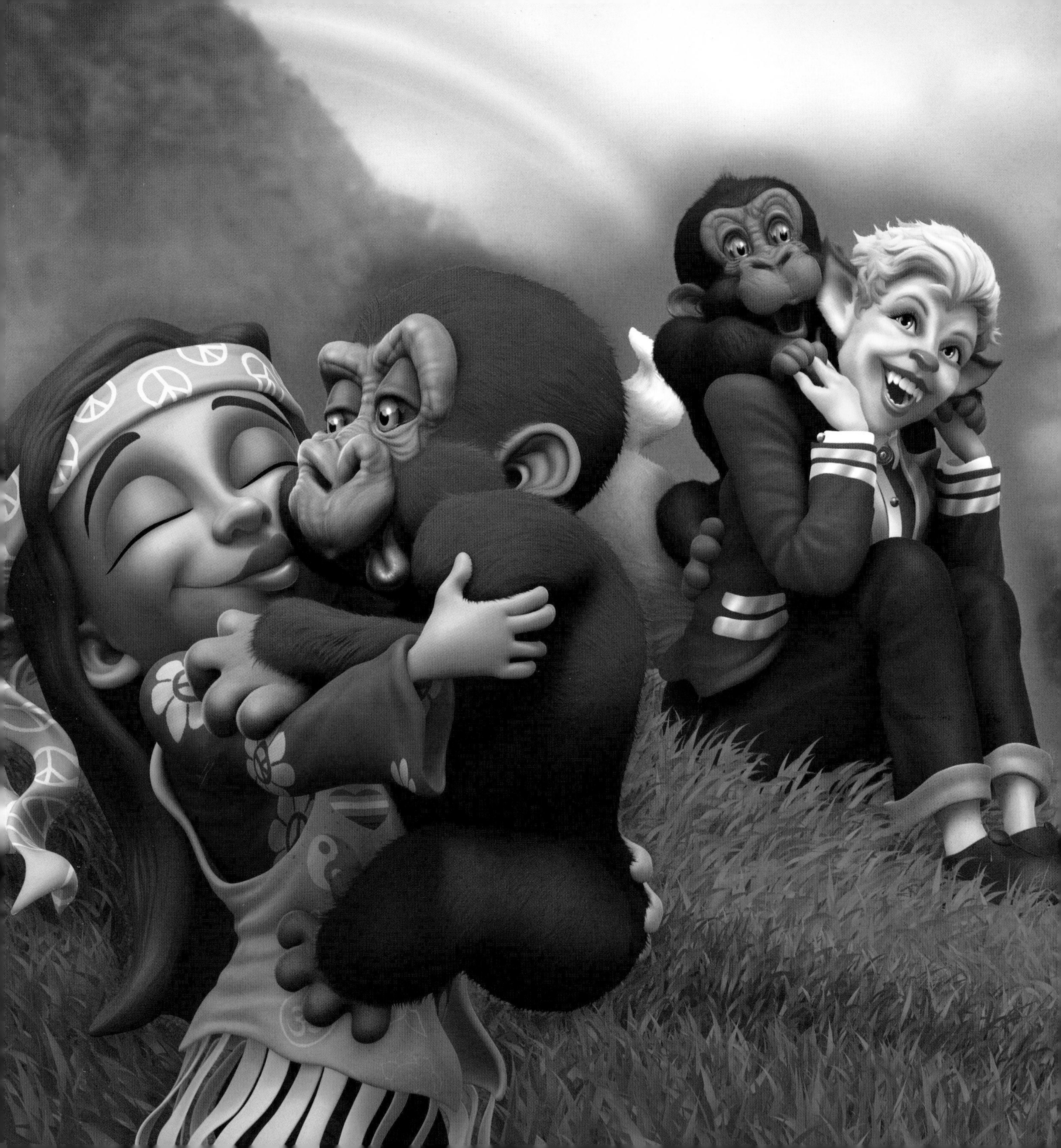

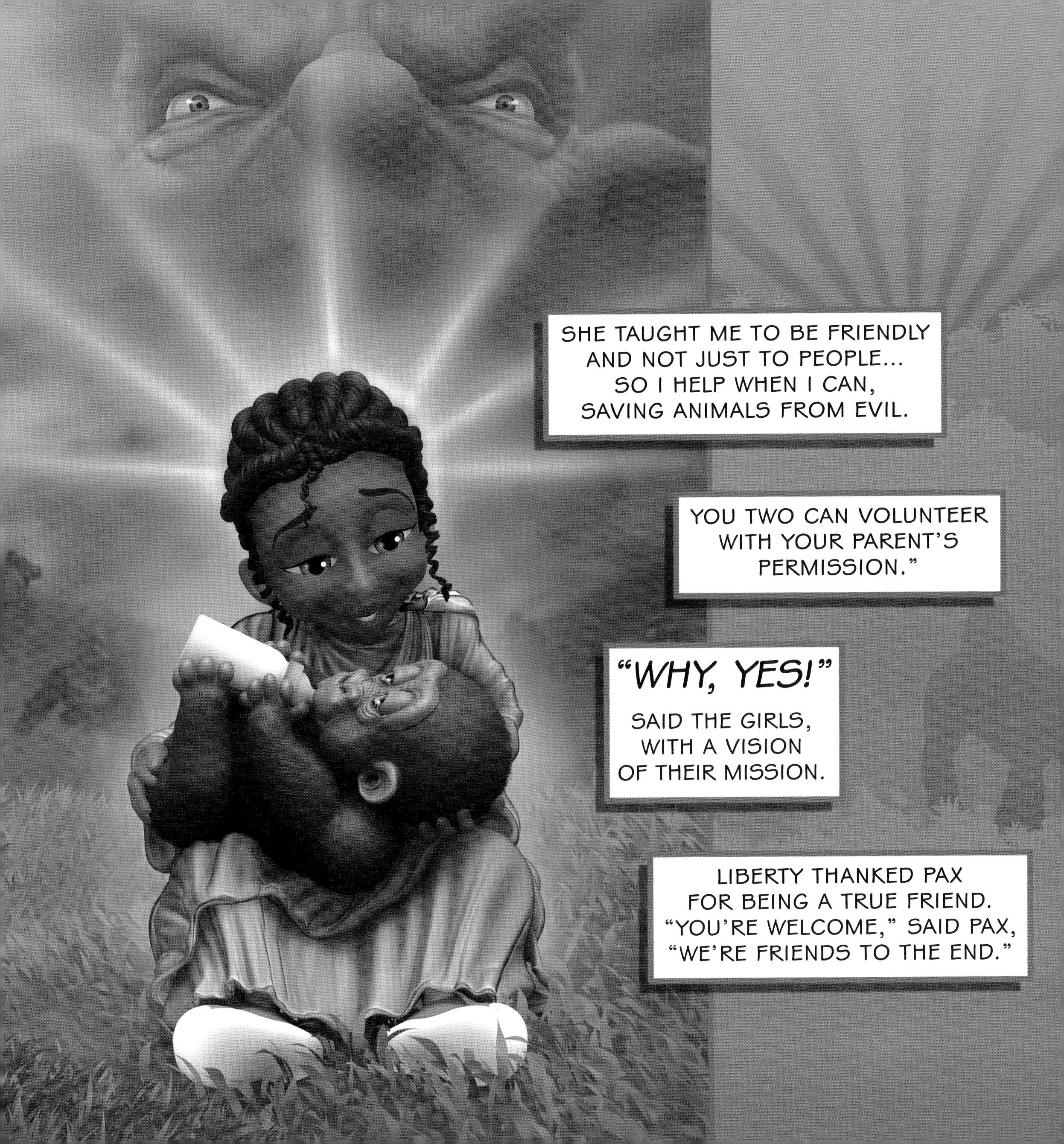
SHE TAUGHT ME TO BE FRIENDLY AND NOT JUST TO PEOPLE... SO I HELP WHEN I CAN, SAVING ANIMALS FROM EVIL.
YOU TWO CAN VOLUNTEER WITH YOUR PARENT'S PERMISSION."
"WHY, YES!"
SAID THE GIRLS, WITH A VISION OF THEIR MISSION.
LIBERTY THANKED PAX FOR BEING A TRUE FRIEND. "YOU'RE WELCOME," SAID PAX, "WE'RE FRIENDS TO THE END."

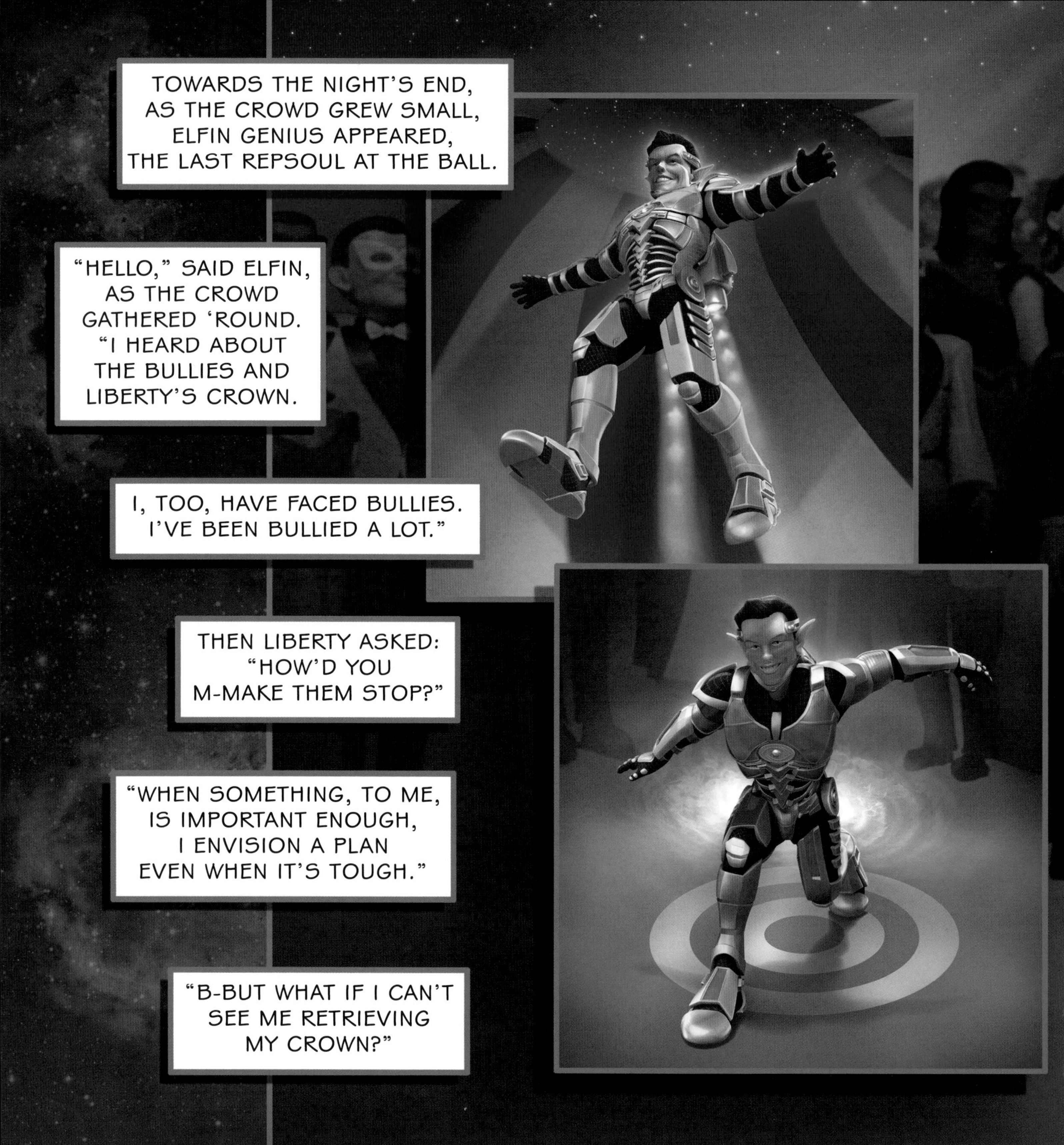
TOWARDS THE NIGHT'S END, AS THE CROWD GREW SMALL, ELFIN GENIUS APPEARED, THE LAST REPSOUL AT THE BALL.
"HELLO," SAID ELFIN, AS THE CROWD GATHERED 'ROUND. "I HEARD ABOUT THE BULLIES AND LIBERTY'S CROWN.
I, TOO, HAVE FACED BULLIES. I'VE BEEN BULLIED A LOT."
THEN LIBERTY ASKED: "HOW'D YOU M-MAKE THEM STOP?"
"WHEN SOMETHING, TO ME, IS IMPORTANT ENOUGH, I ENVISION A PLAN EVEN WHEN IT'S TOUGH."
"B-BUT WHAT IF I CAN'T SEE ME RETRIEVING MY CROWN?"

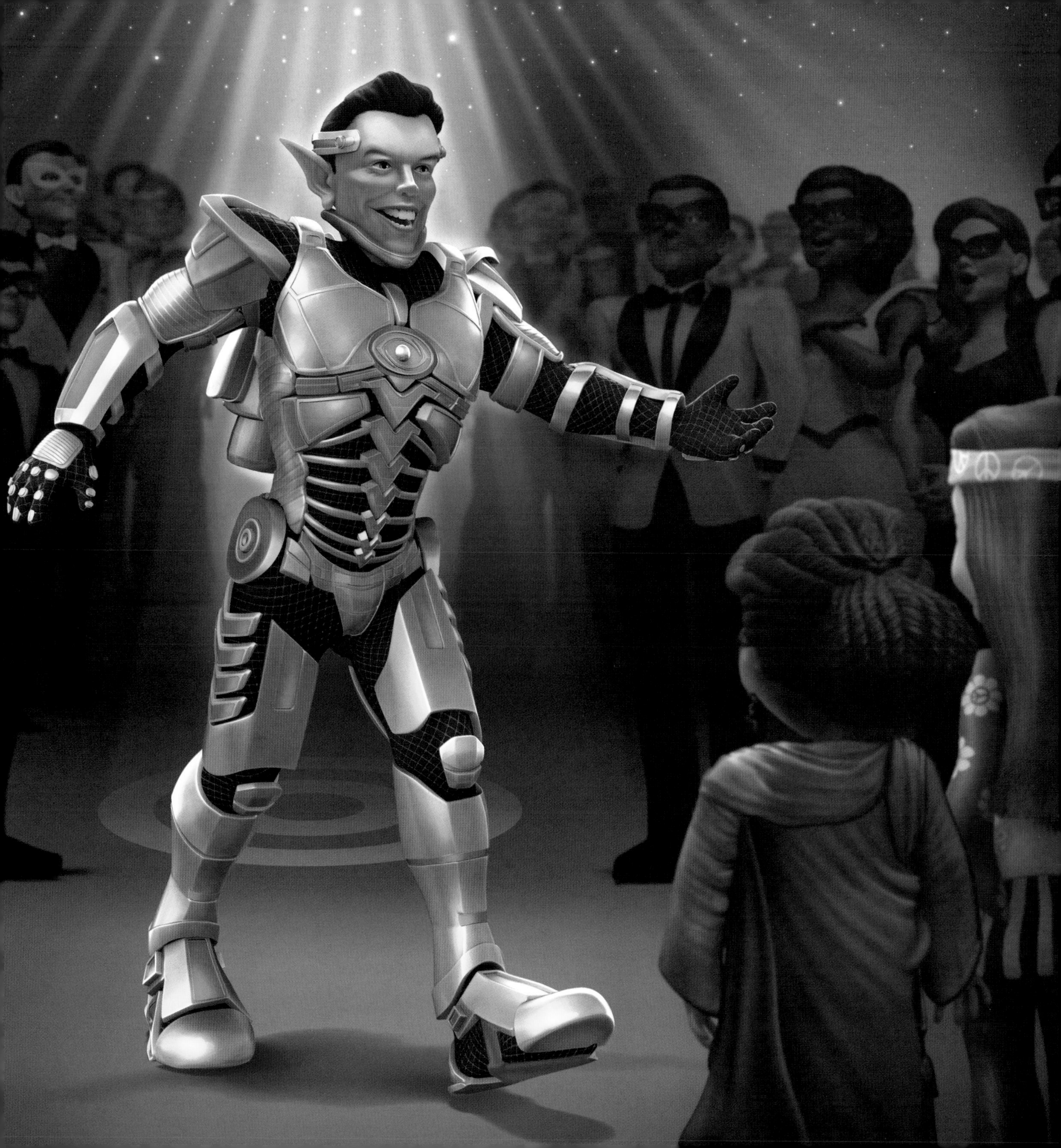

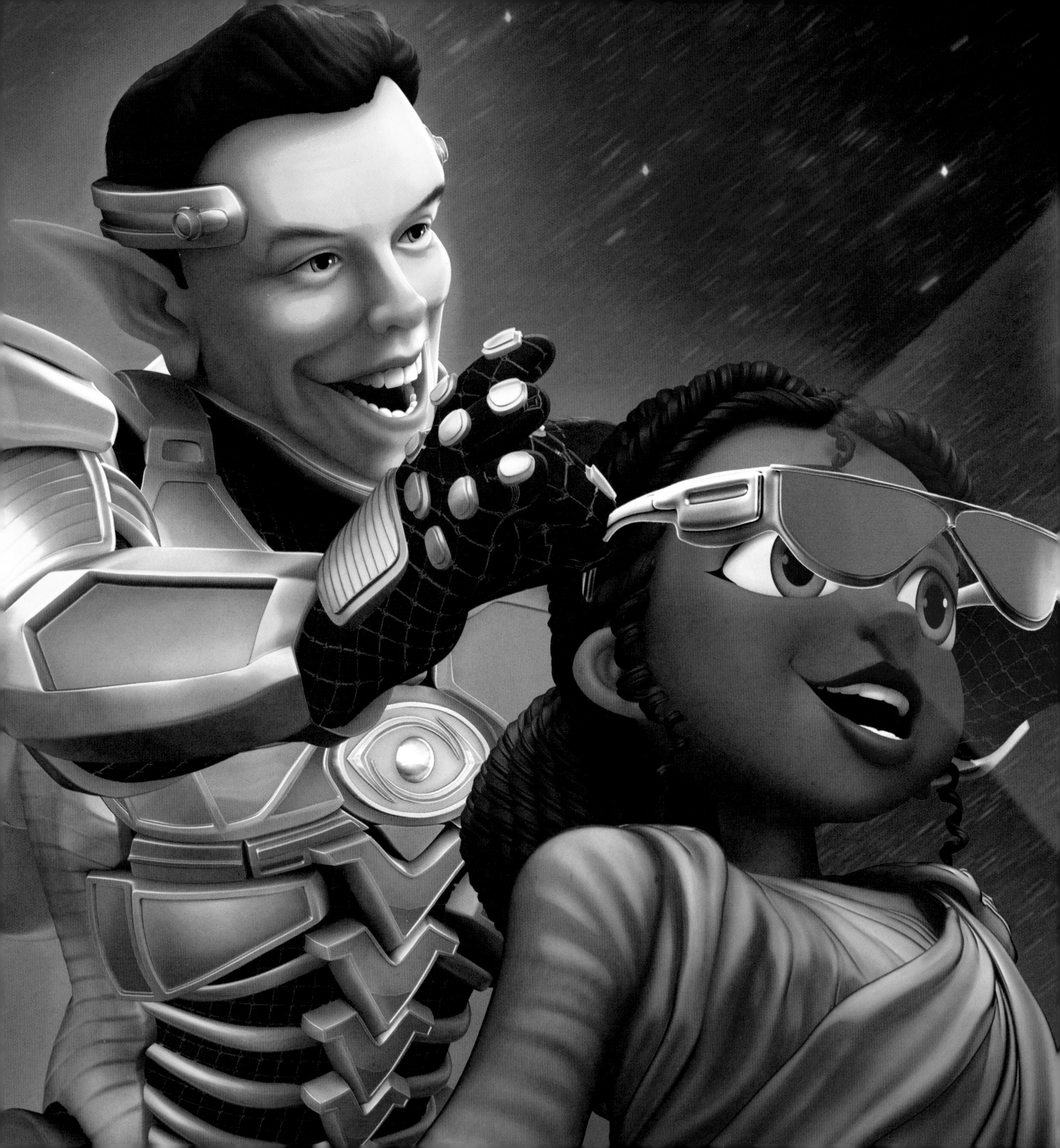

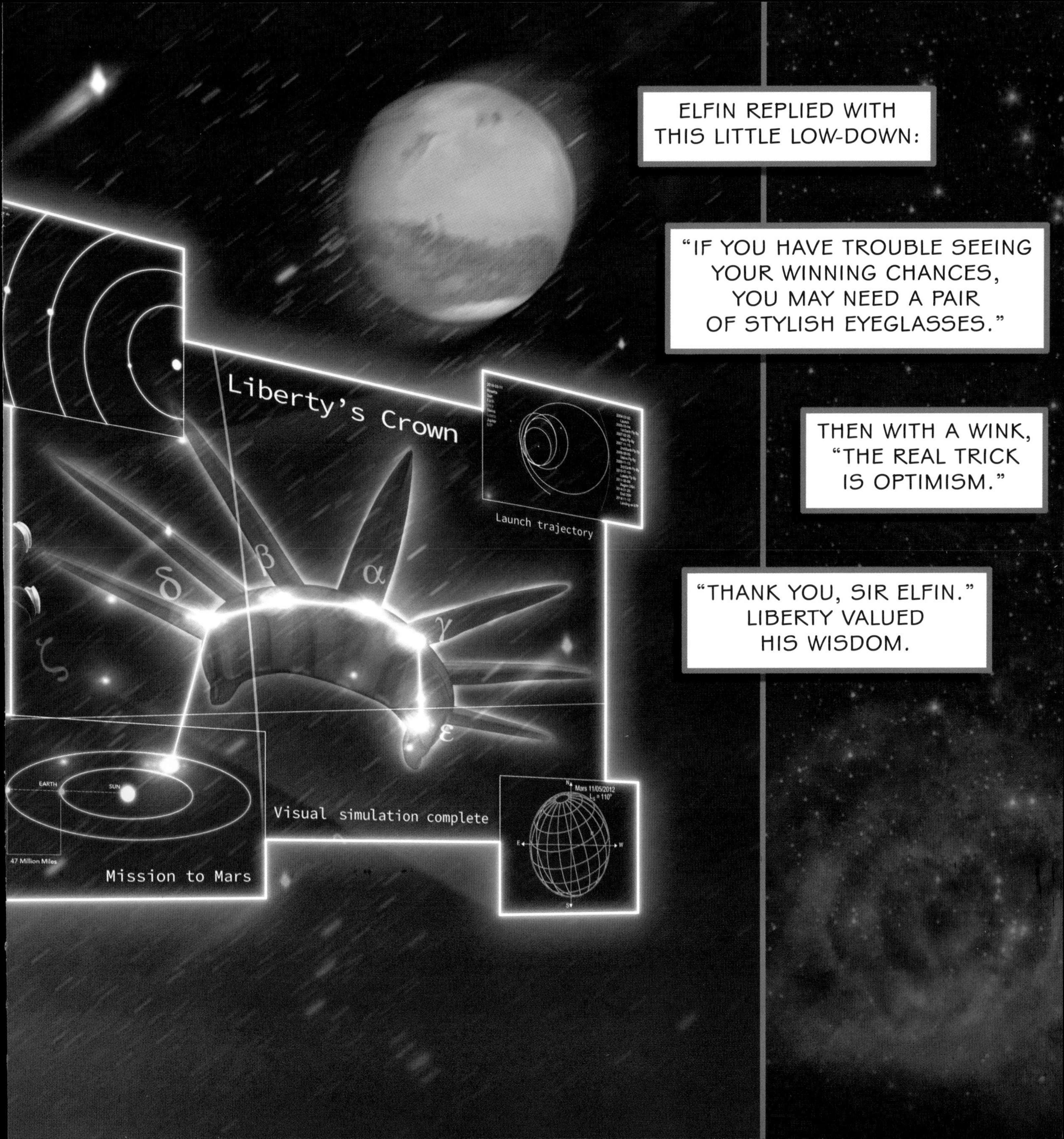
Liberty's Crown
Launch trajectory
Visual simulation complete
Mission to Mars
47 Million Miles
EARTH
SUN
Mars 11/05/2012
ELFIN REPLIED WITH THIS LITTLE LOW-DOWN:
"IF YOU HAVE TROUBLE SEEING YOUR WINNING CHANCES, YOU MAY NEED A PAIR OF STYLISH EYEGLASSES."
THEN WITH A WINK, "THE REAL TRICK IS OPTIMISM."
"THANK YOU, SIR ELFIN." LIBERTY VALUED HIS WISDOM.

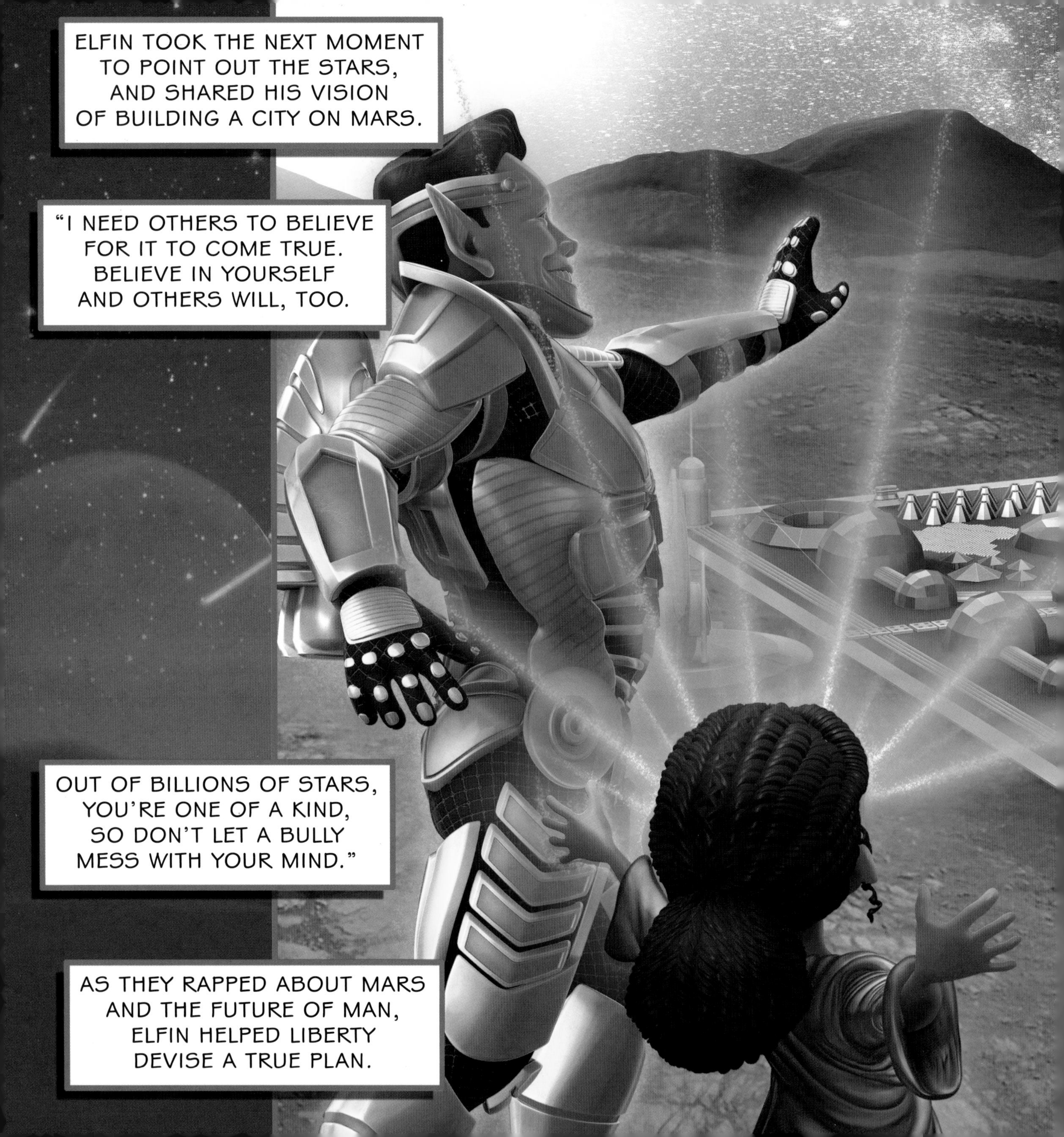

ELFIN TOOK THE NEXT MOMENT
TO POINT OUT THE STARS,
AND SHARED HIS VISION
OF BUILDING A CITY ON MARS.

“I NEED OTHERS TO BELIEVE
FOR IT TO COME TRUE.
BELIEVE IN YOURSELF
AND OTHERS WILL, TOO.

OUT OF BILLIONS OF STARS,
YOU’RE ONE OF A KIND,
SO DON’T LET A BULLY
MESS WITH YOUR MIND.”

AS THEY RAPPED ABOUT MARS
AND THE FUTURE OF MAN,
ELFIN HELPED LIBERTY
DEVISE A TRUE PLAN.

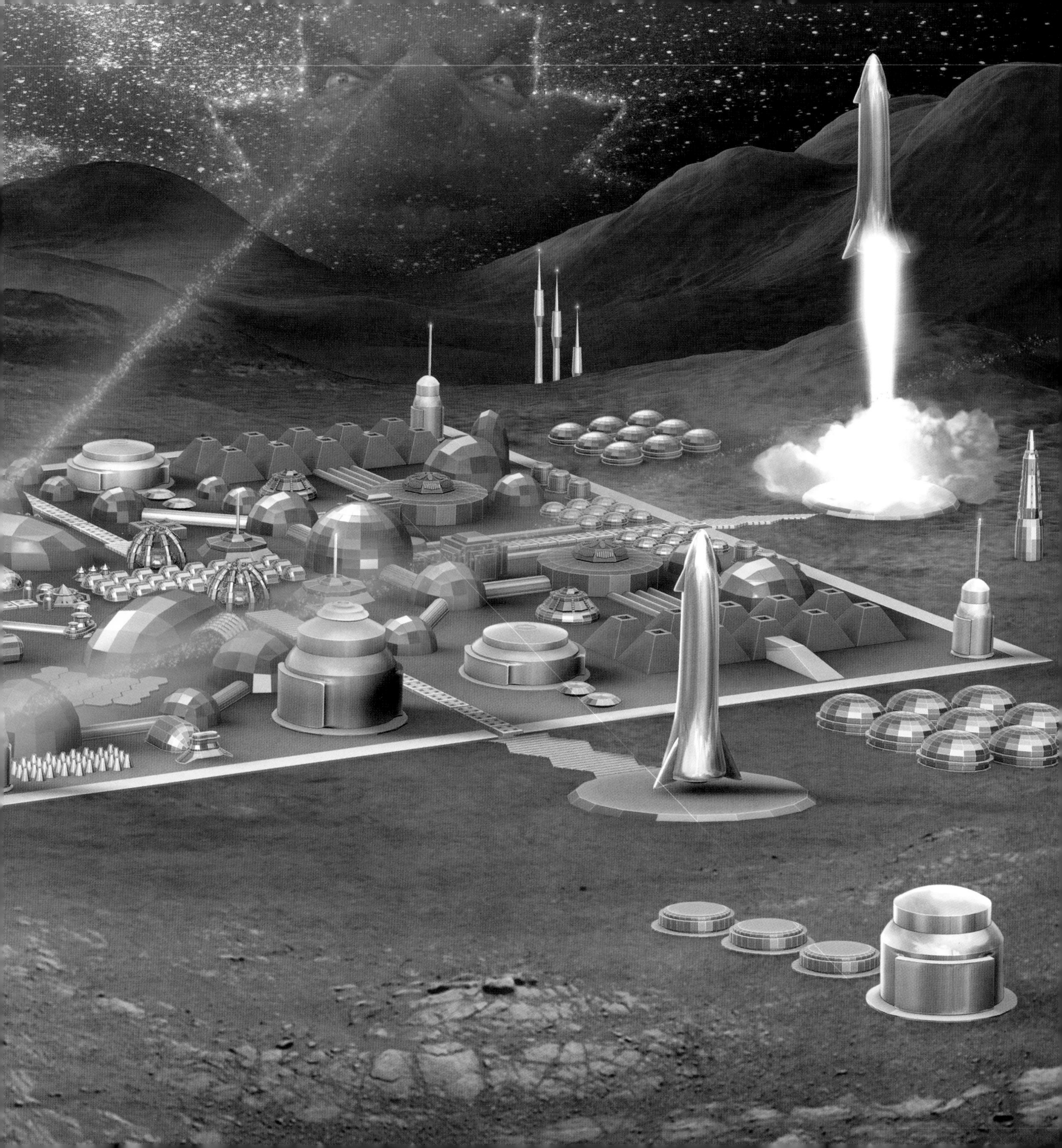

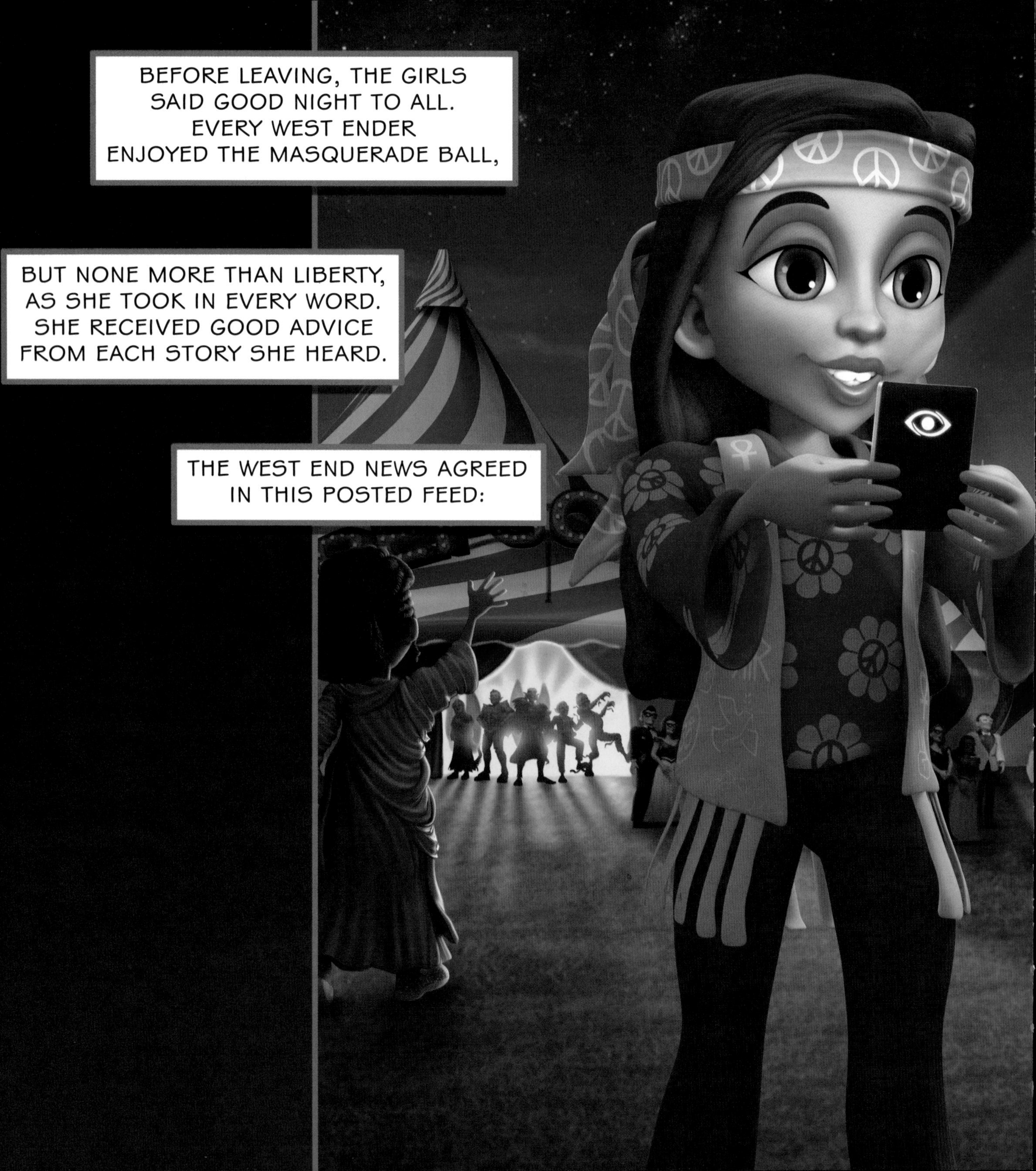
BEFORE LEAVING, THE GIRLS SAID GOOD NIGHT TO ALL. EVERY WEST ENDER ENJOYED THE MASQUERADE BALL,
BUT NONE MORE THAN LIBERTY, AS SHE TOOK IN EVERY WORD. SHE RECEIVED GOOD ADVICE FROM EACH STORY SHE HEARD.
THE WEST END NEWS AGREED IN THIS POSTED FEED:

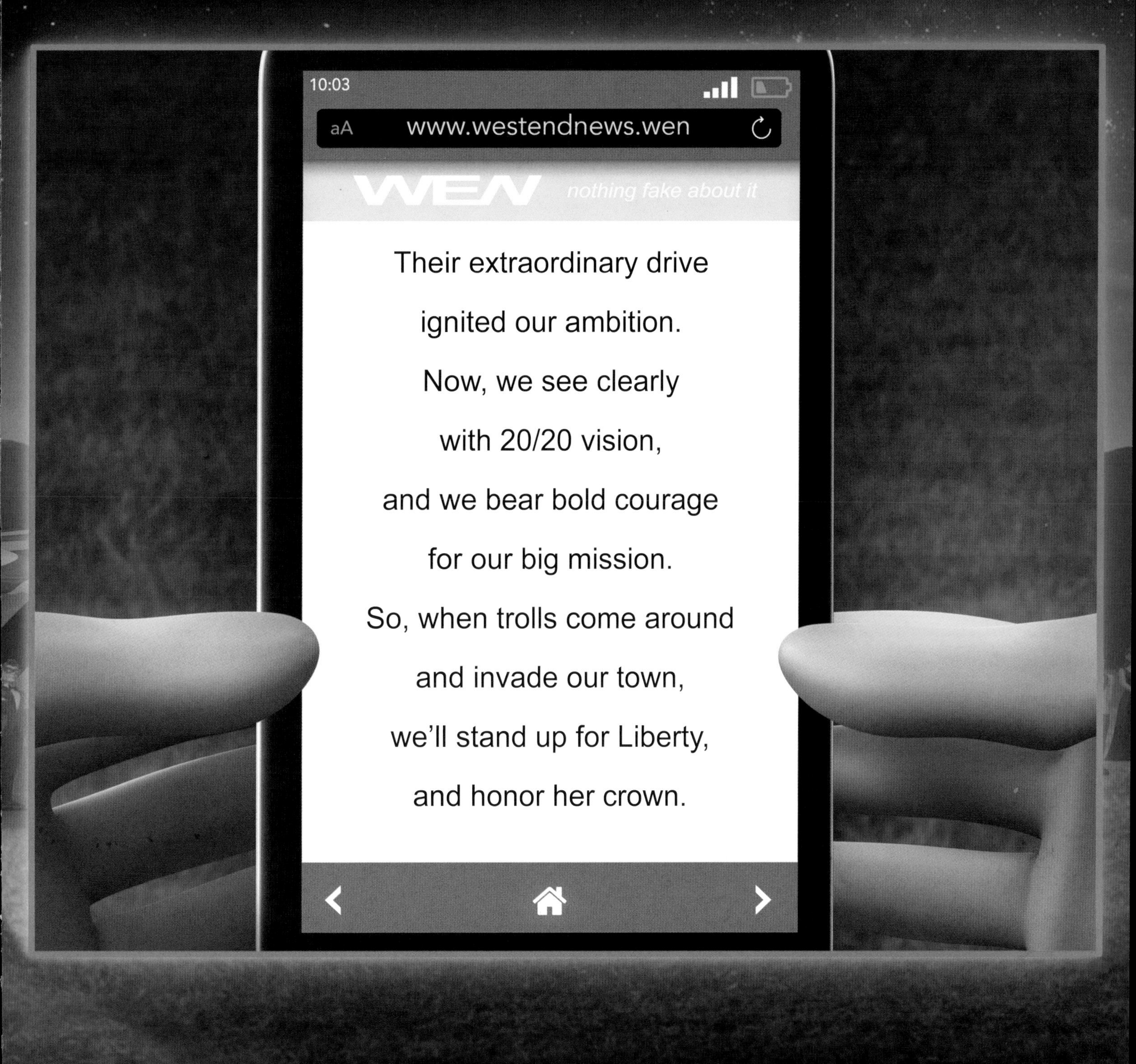
10:03
aA www.westendnews.wen
WEN nothing fake about it
Their extraordinary drive
ignited our ambition.
Now, we see clearly
with 20/20 vision,
and we bear bold courage
for our big mission.
So, when trolls come around
and invade our town,
we'll stand up for Liberty,
and honor her crown.

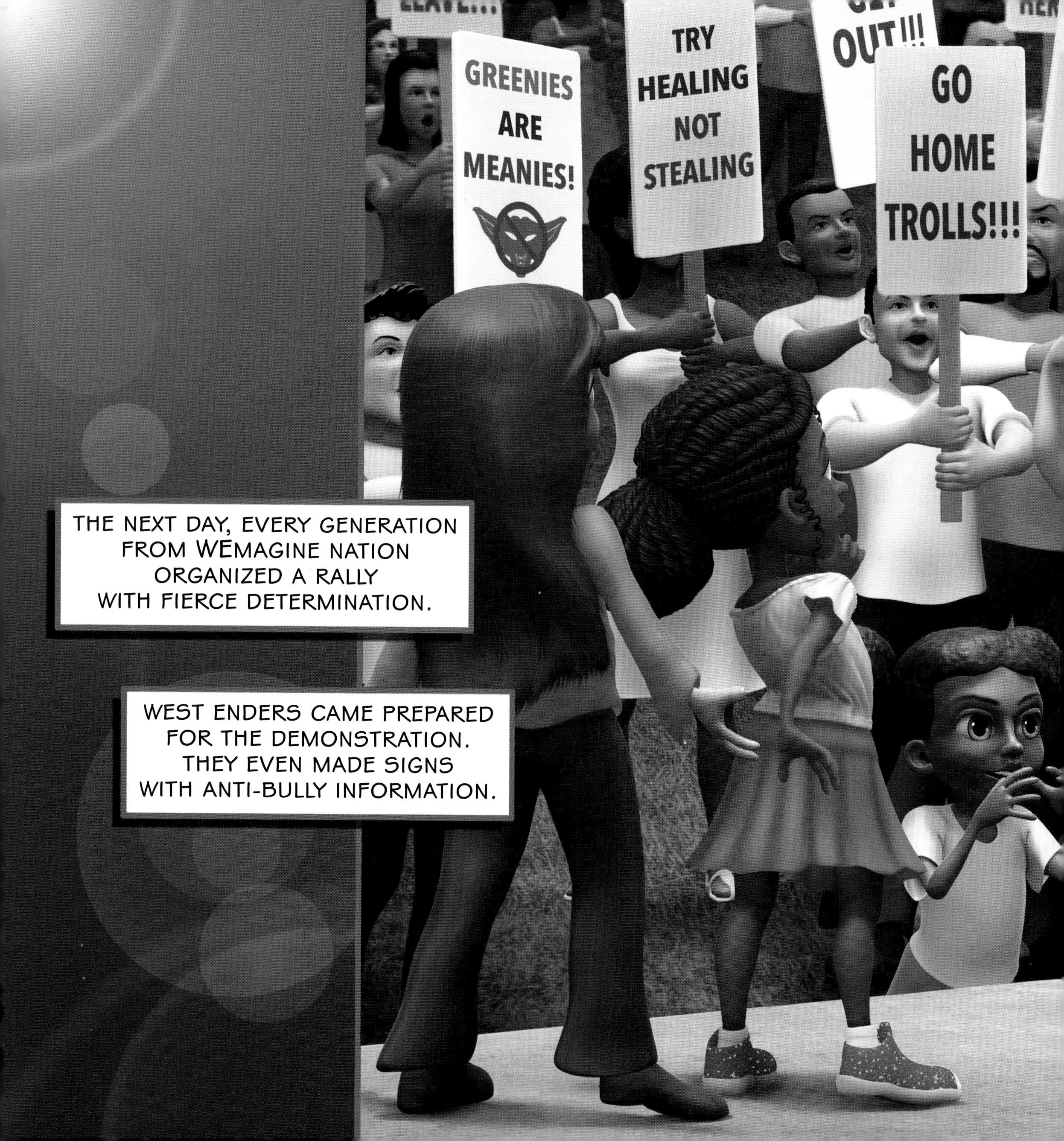
THE NEXT DAY, EVERY GENERATION FROM WEMAGINE NATION ORGANIZED A RALLY WITH FIERCE DETERMINATION.
WEST ENDERS CAME PREPARED FOR THE DEMONSTRATION. THEY EVEN MADE SIGNS WITH ANTI-BULLY INFORMATION.
GREENIES ARE MEANIES!
TRY HEALING NOT STEALING
OUT!!!
GO HOME TROLLS!!!

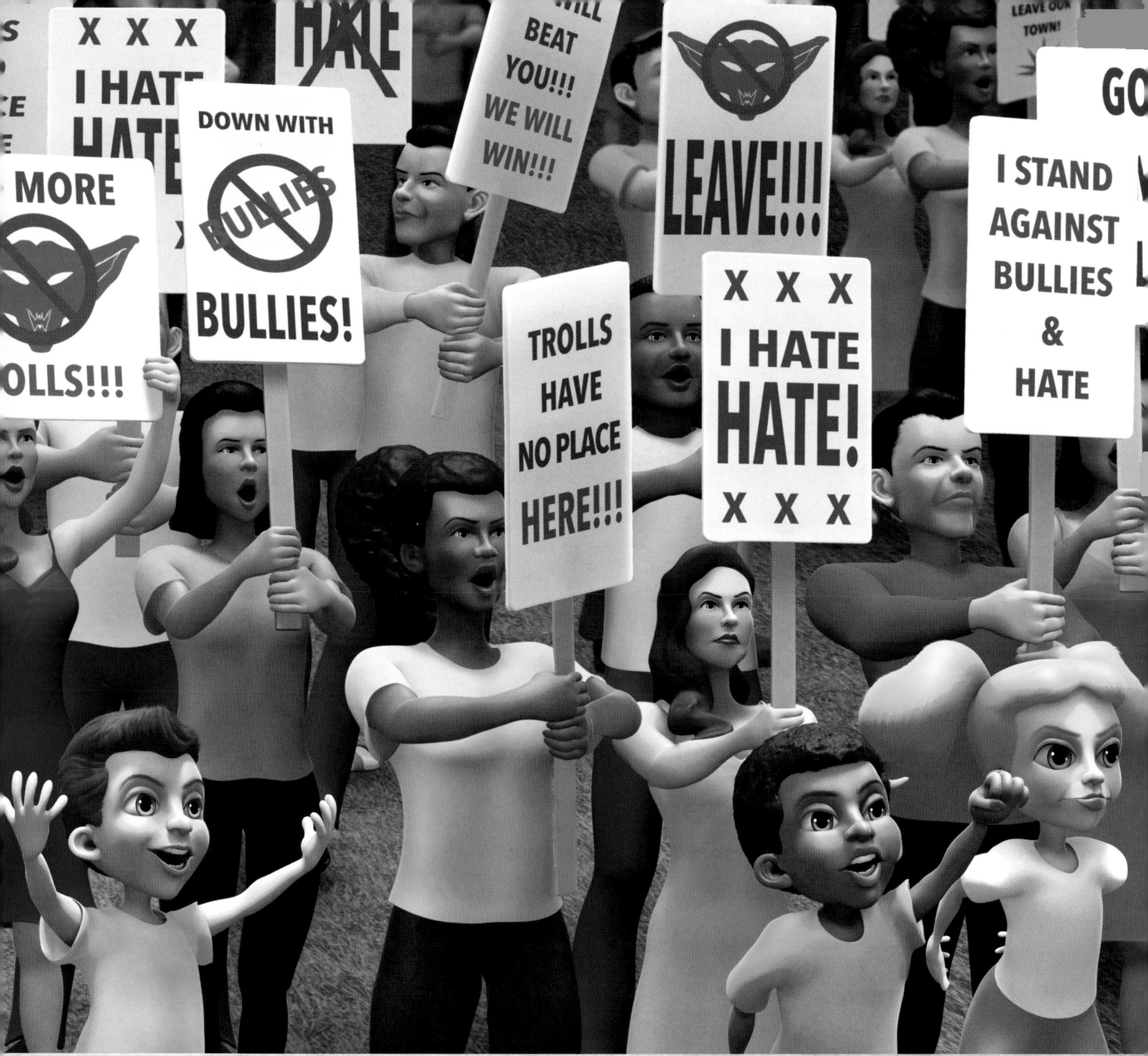
X X X
I HATE
DOWN WITH
BULLIES
BULLIES!
MORE
BEAT
YOU!!!
WE WILL
WIN!!!
LEAVE!!!
LEAVE OUR
TOWN!
TROLLS
HAVE
NO PLACE
HERE!!!
X X X
I HATE
HATE!
X X X
I STAND
AGAINST
BULLIES
&
HATE

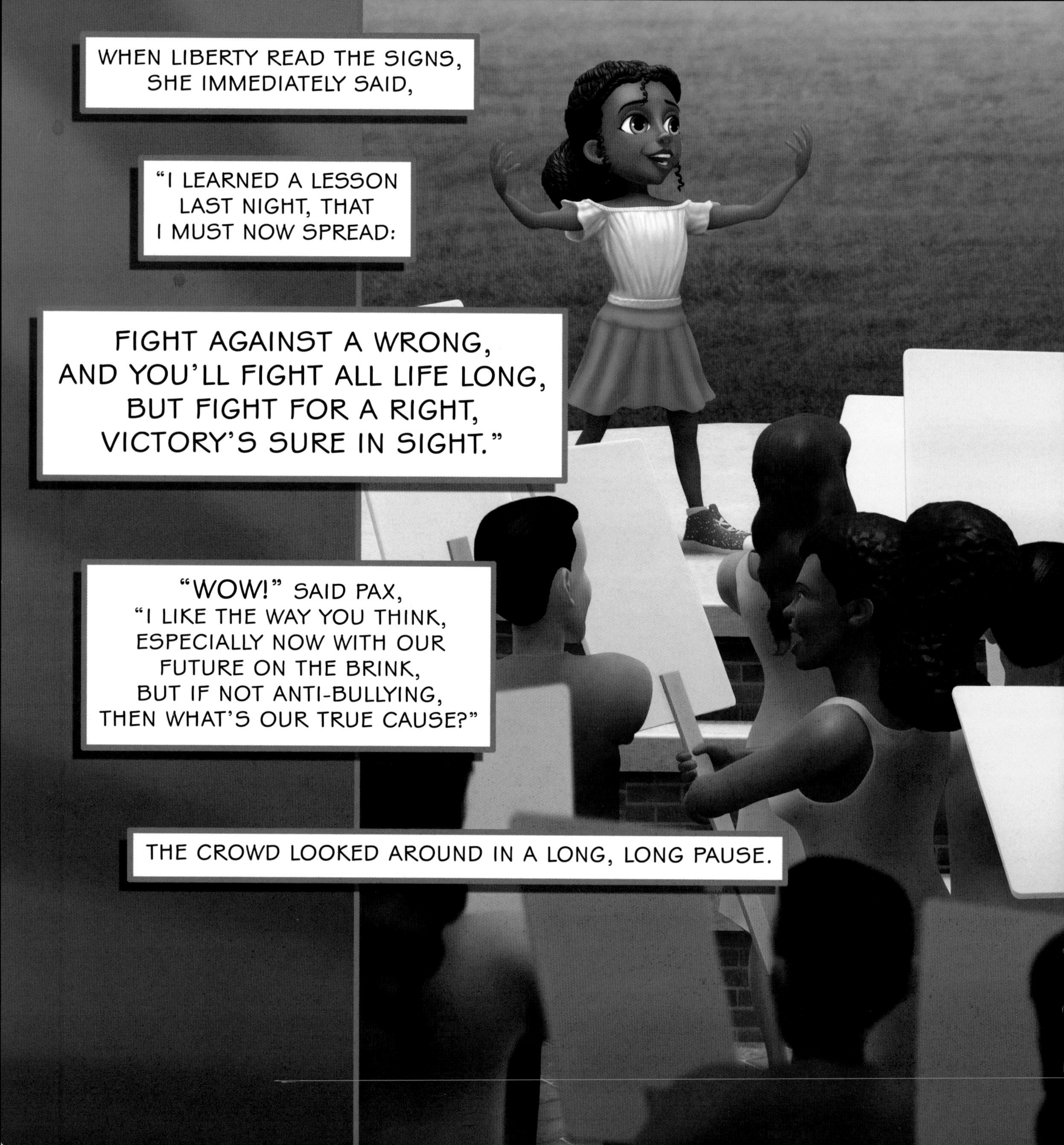
WHEN LIBERTY READ THE SIGNS, SHE IMMEDIATELY SAID,
"I LEARNED A LESSON LAST NIGHT, THAT I MUST NOW SPREAD:
FIGHT AGAINST A WRONG, AND YOU'LL FIGHT ALL LIFE LONG, BUT FIGHT FOR A RIGHT, VICTORY'S SURE IN SIGHT."
"WOW!" SAID PAX, "I LIKE THE WAY YOU THINK, ESPECIALLY NOW WITH OUR FUTURE ON THE BRINK, BUT IF NOT ANTI-BULLYING, THEN WHAT'S OUR TRUE CAUSE?"
THE CROWD LOOKED AROUND IN A LONG, LONG PAUSE.

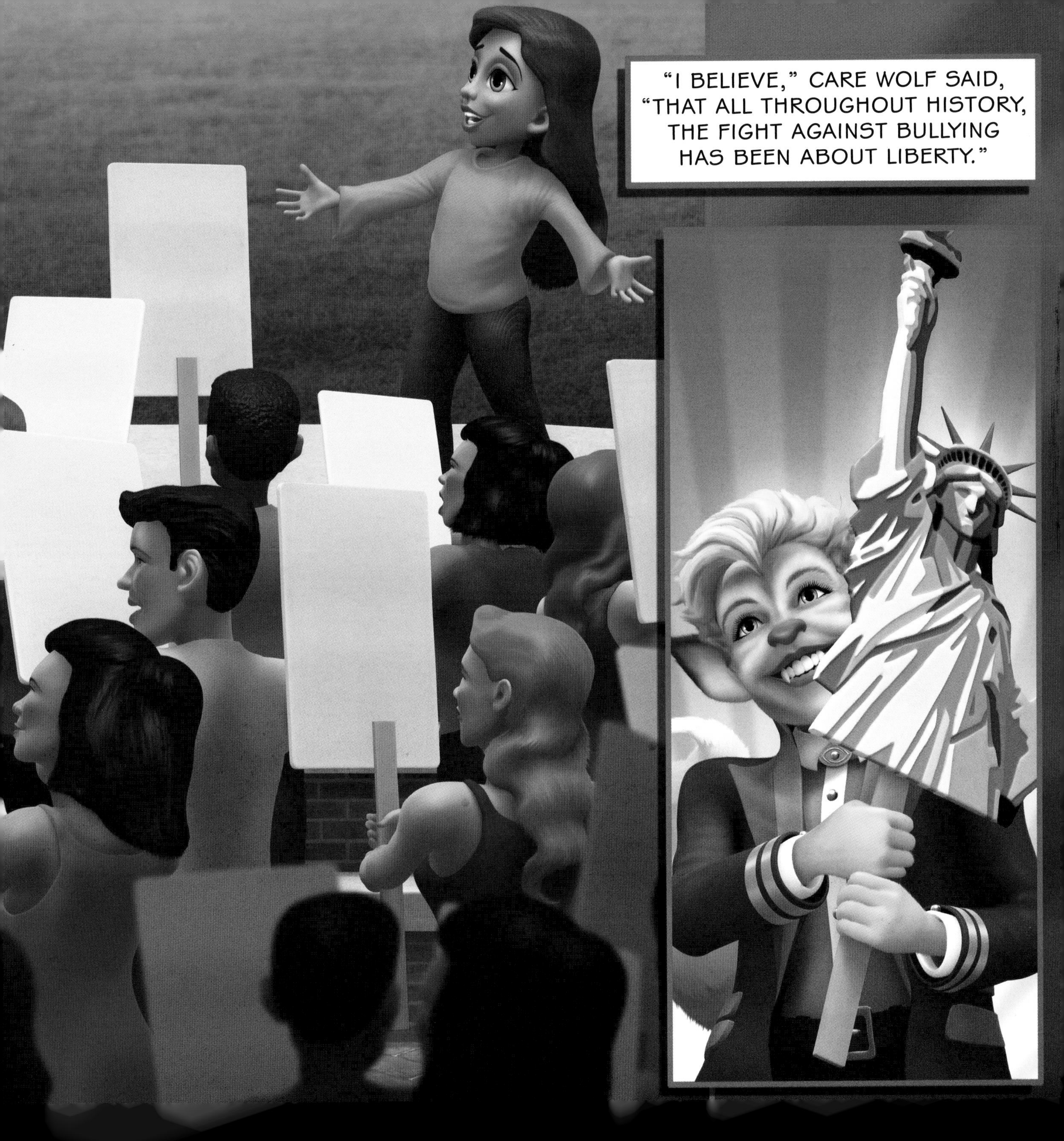
"I BELIEVE," CARE WOLF SAID, "THAT ALL THROUGHOUT HISTORY, THE FIGHT AGAINST BULLYING HAS BEEN ABOUT LIBERTY."

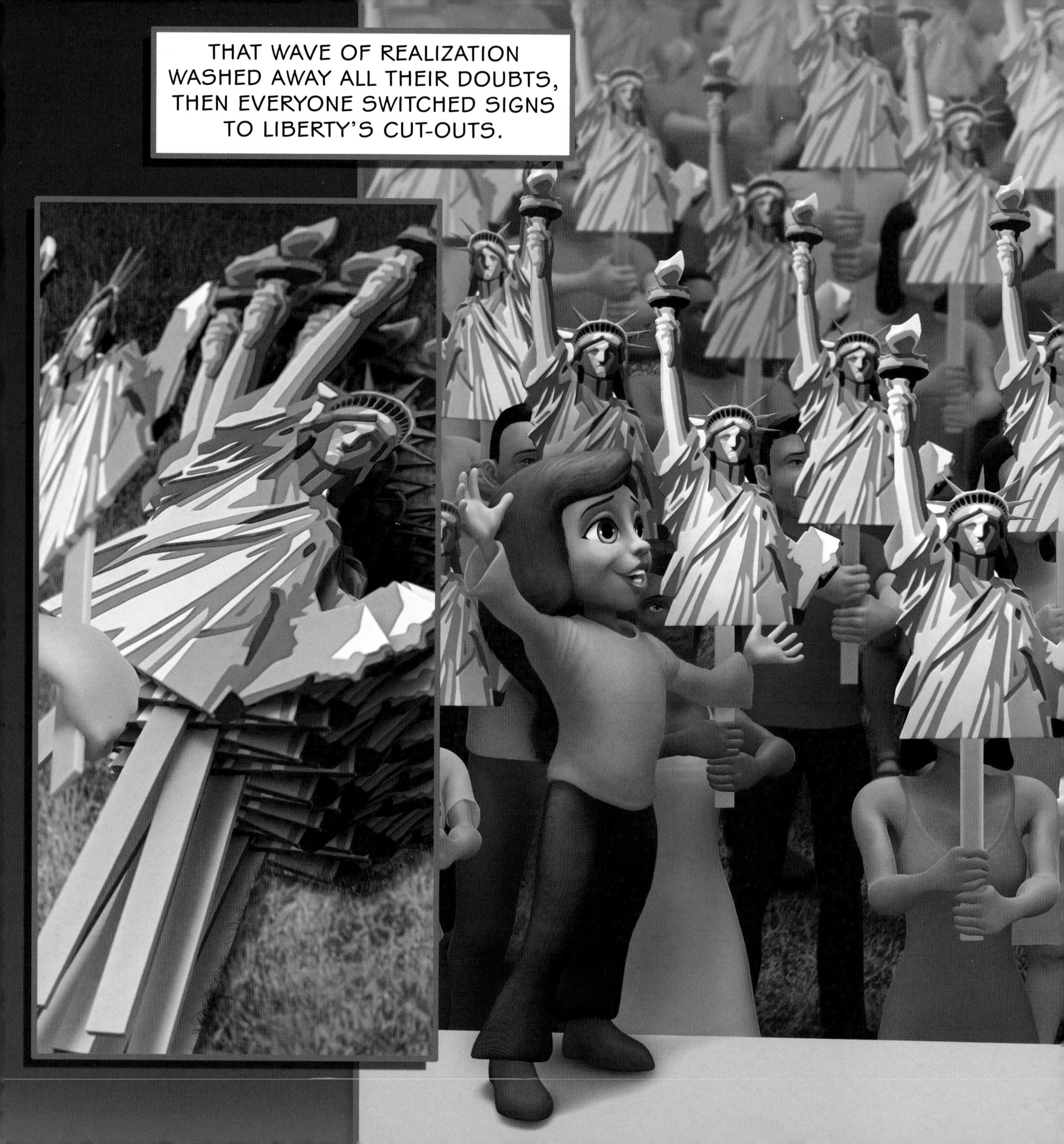
THAT WAVE OF REALIZATION WASHED AWAY ALL THEIR DOUBTS, THEN EVERYONE SWITCHED SIGNS TO LIBERTY'S CUT-OUTS.

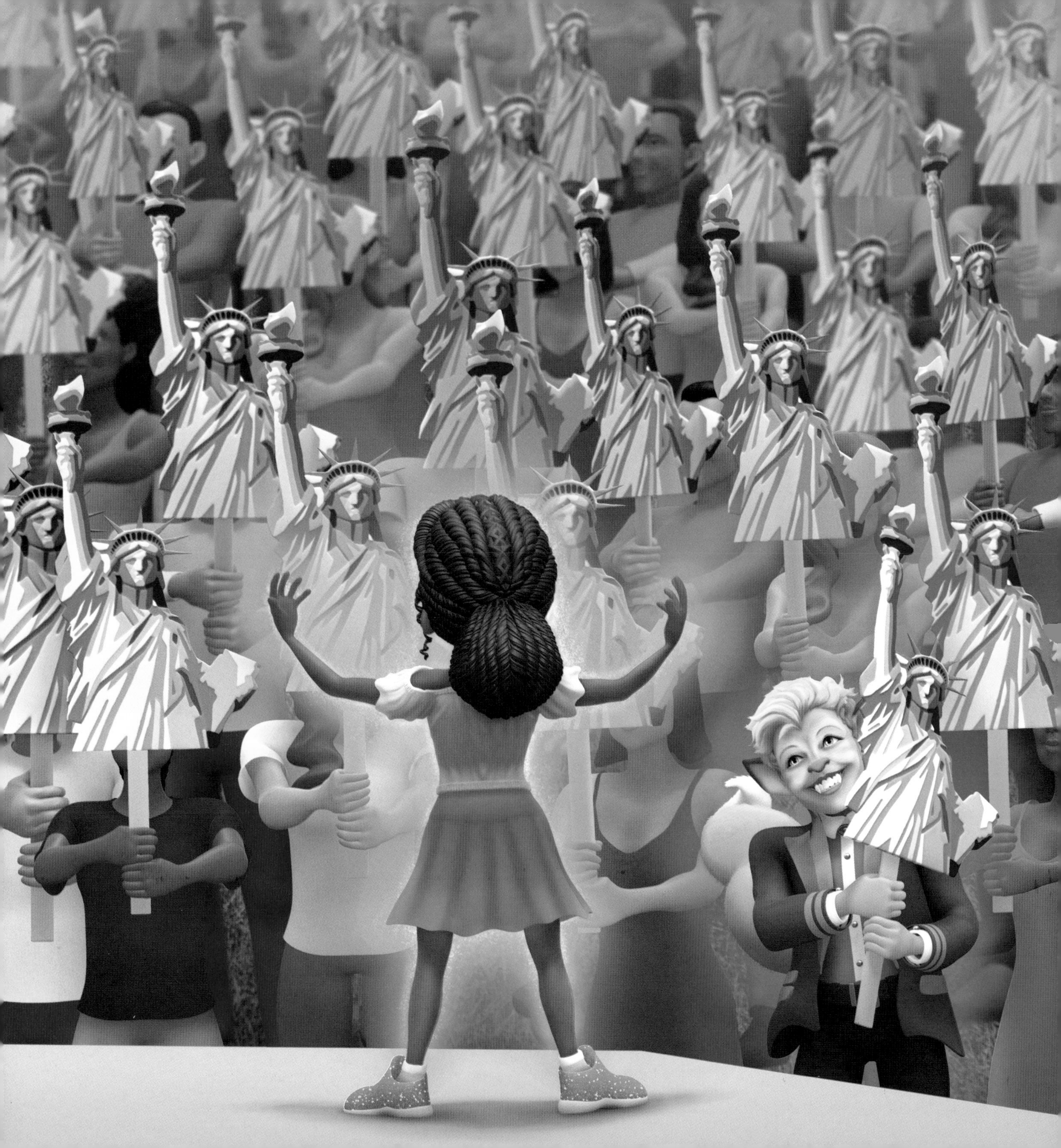

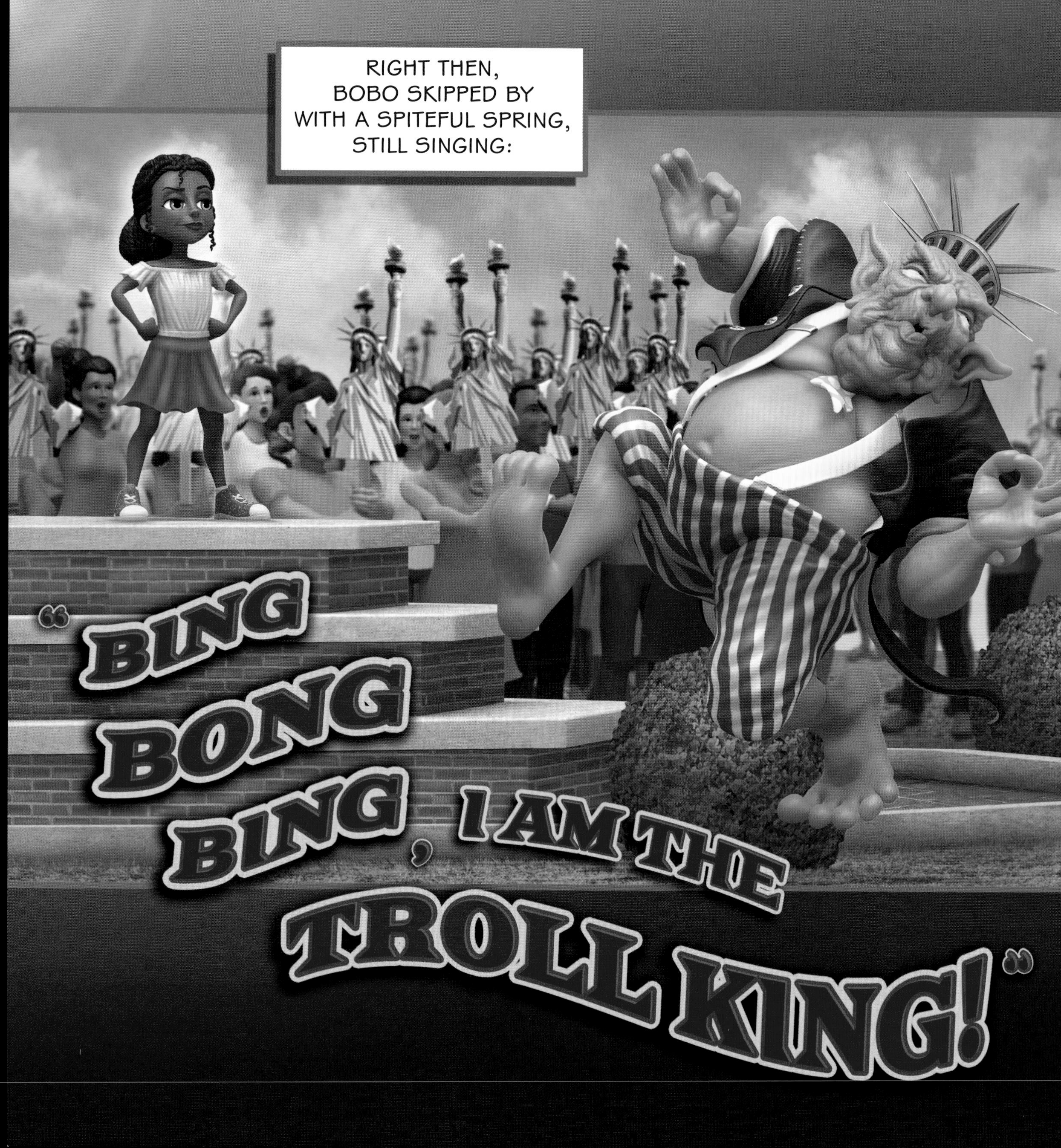
RIGHT THEN, BOBO SKIPPED BY WITH A SPITEFUL SPRING, STILL SINGING:
"BING BONG BING, I AM THE TROLL KING!"

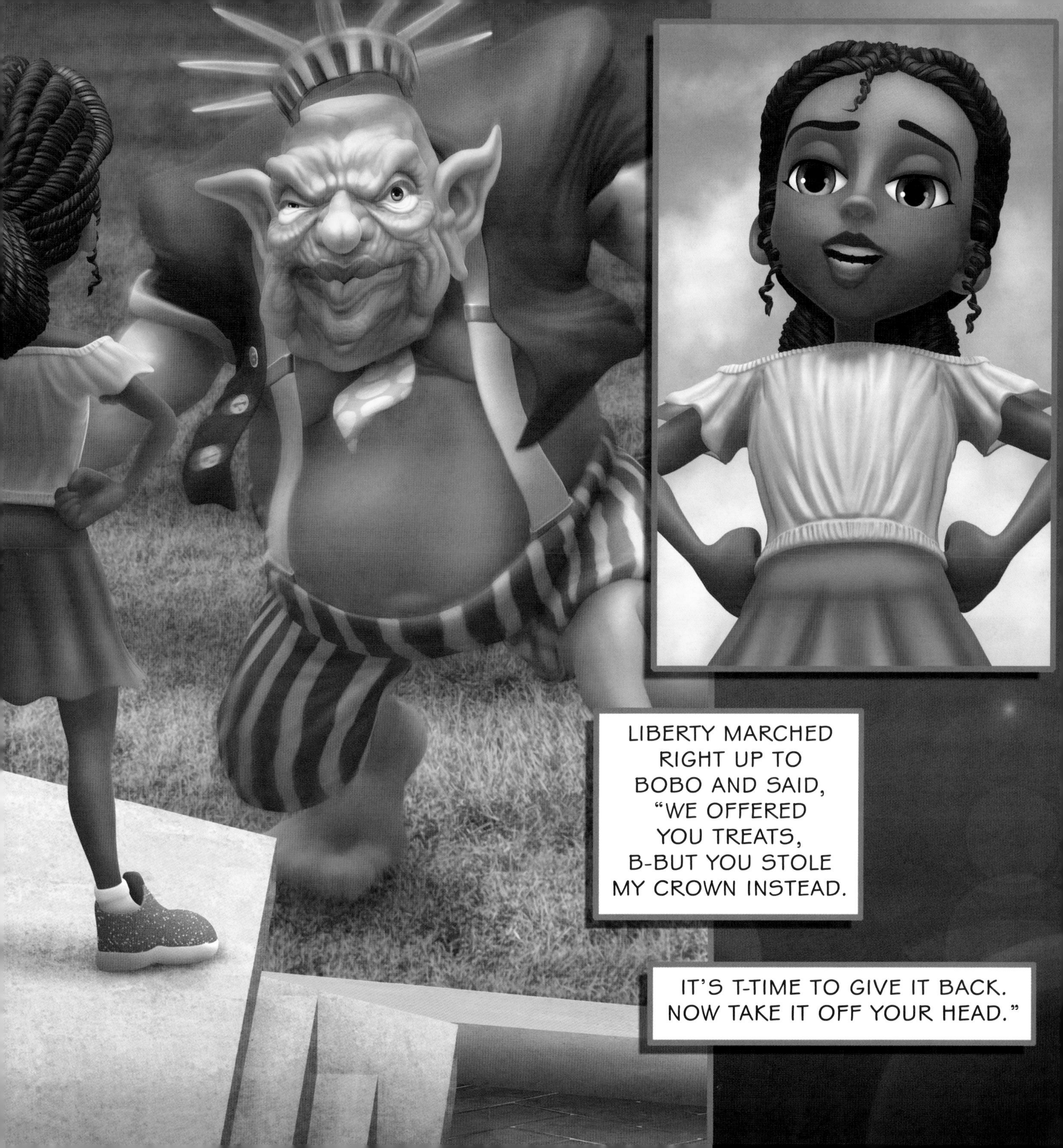

LIBERTY MARCHED RIGHT UP TO BOBO AND SAID, “WE OFFERED YOU TREATS, B-BUT YOU STOLE MY CROWN INSTEAD.
IT’S T-TIME TO GIVE IT BACK. NOW TAKE IT OFF YOUR HEAD.”

"SHOW ME SOME RESPECT
OR YOUR PRECIOUS CROWN IS DEAD!

THIS THING IS MADE OF PLASTIC
AND I CAN SNAP IT JUST LIKE THAT.
YOU LOST IT. I FOUND IT.
IT'S MINE AND THAT'S A FACT!

YOU COULDN'T HOLD ONTO IT.
YOU DON'T KNOW WHAT TO DO.
AS A MATTER OF FACT,
I HAVE A NICKNAME FOR YOU.

I HAD SOME FUN WITH A RHYME OR TWO,

SLIPPERY
LIBERTY!"

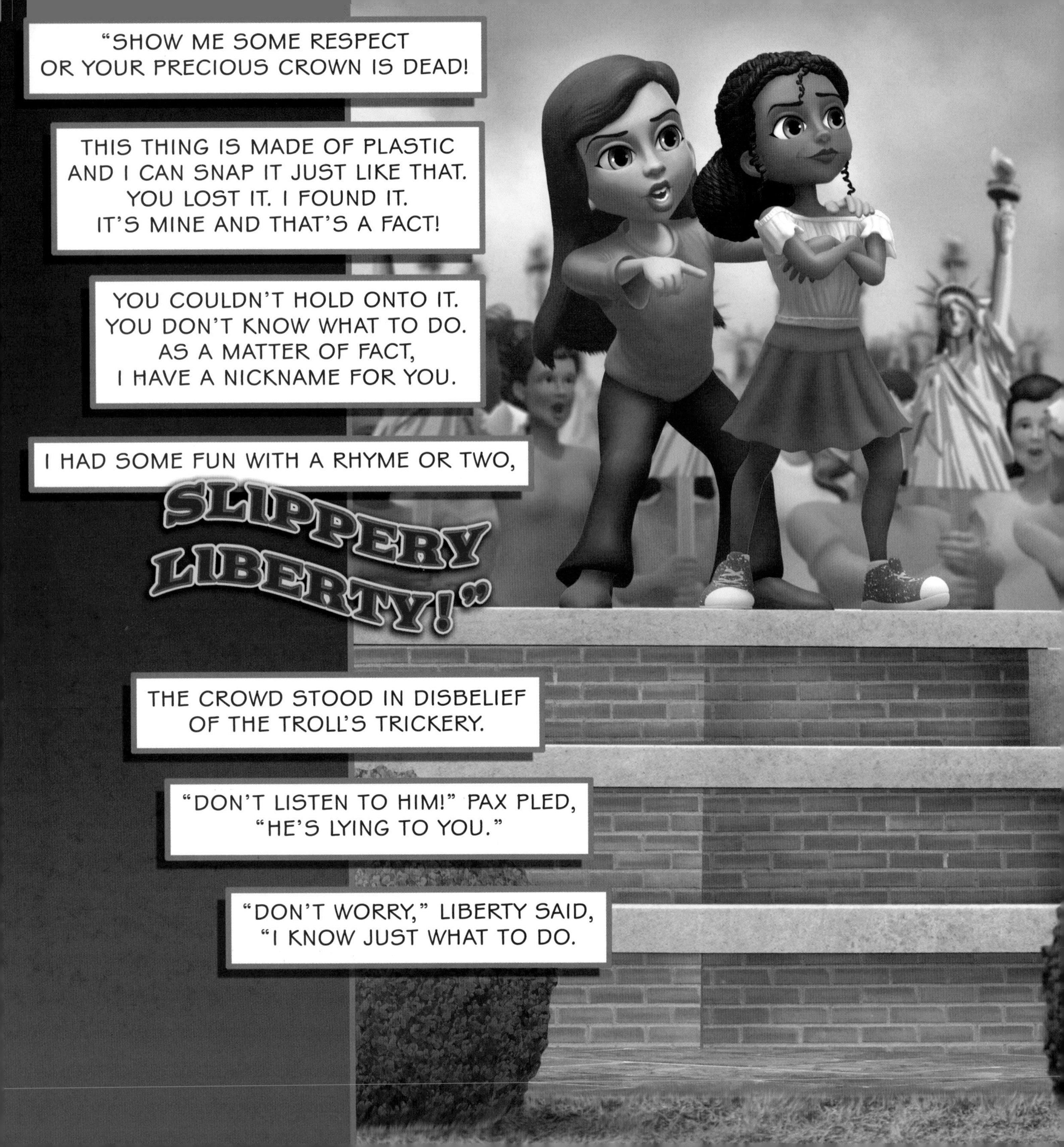

THE CROWD STOOD IN DISBELIEF
OF THE TROLL'S TRICKERY.

"DON'T LISTEN TO HIM!" PAX PLED,
"HE'S LYING TO YOU."

"DON'T WORRY," LIBERTY SAID,
"I KNOW JUST WHAT TO DO.

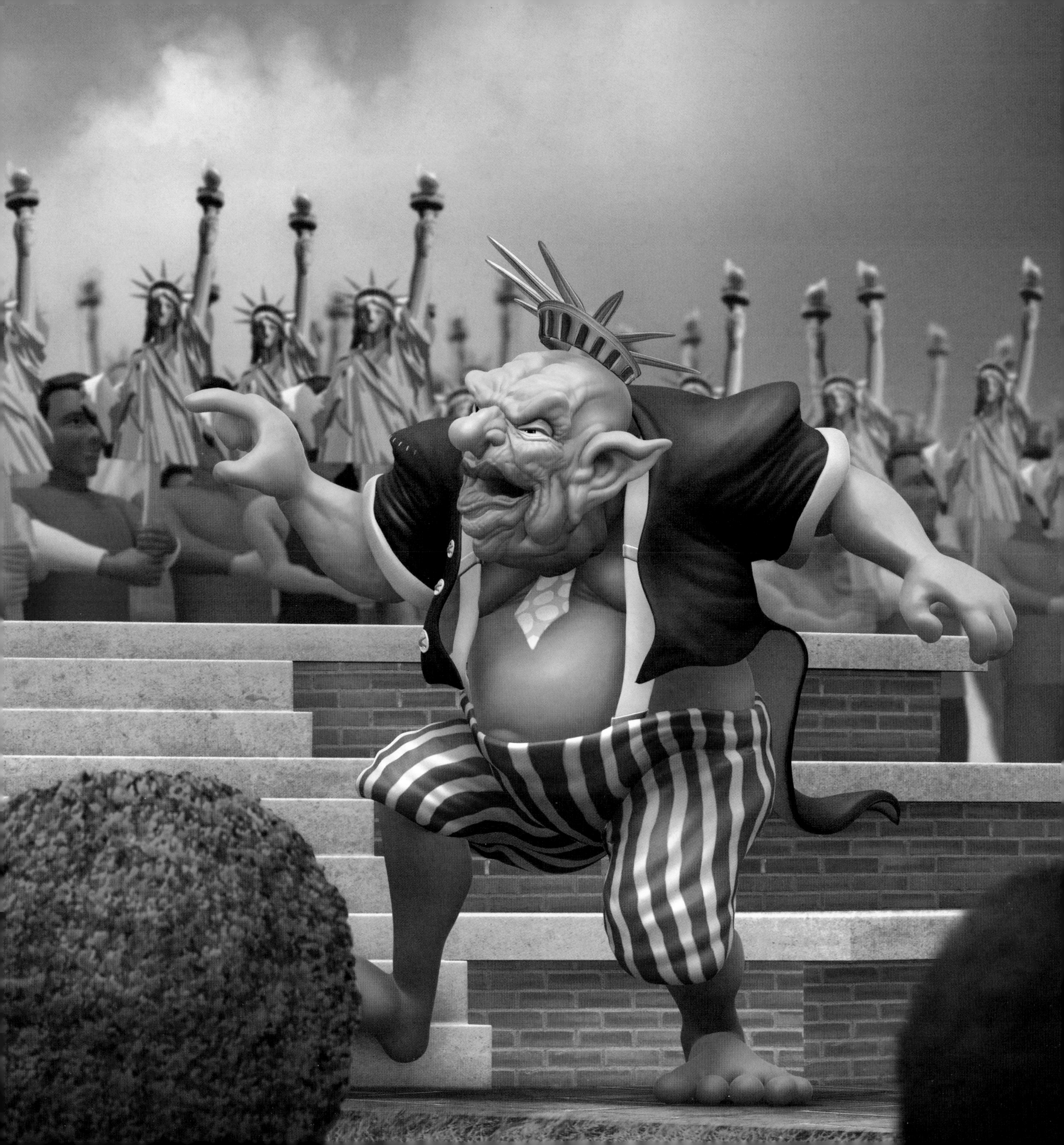

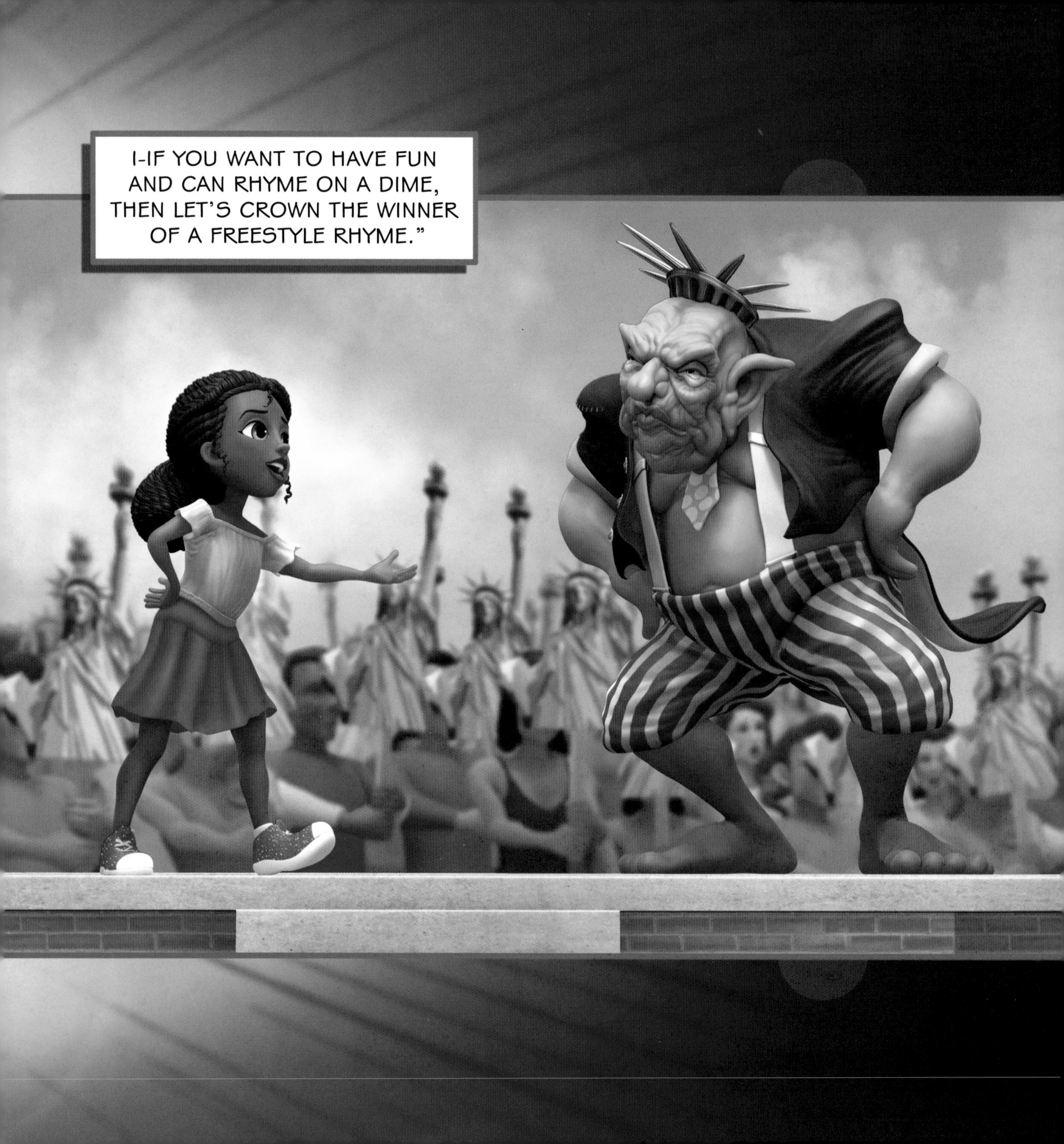
I-IF YOU WANT TO HAVE FUN
AND CAN RHYME ON A DIME,
THEN LET'S CROWN THE WINNER
OF A FREESTYLE RHYME."

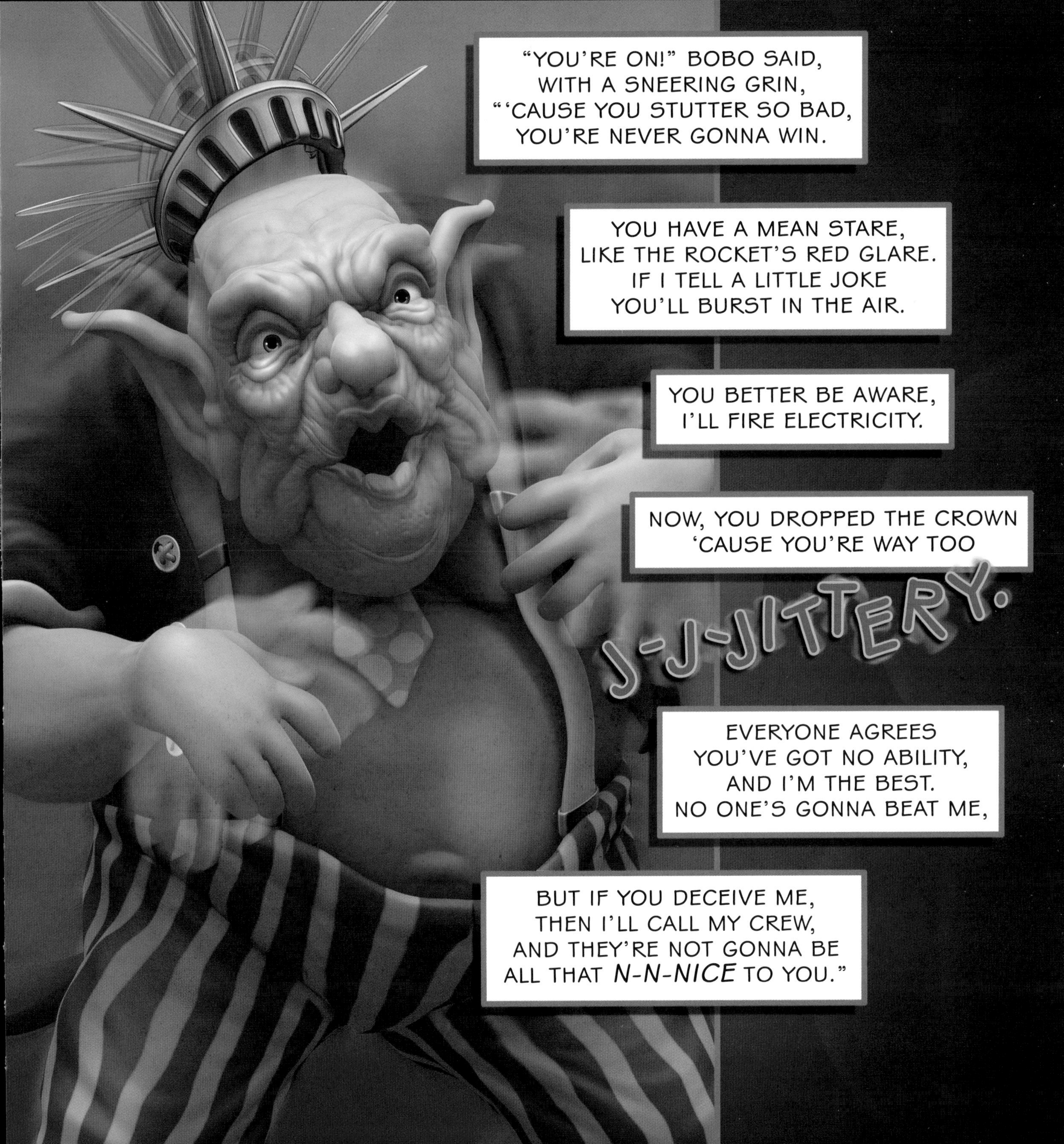
"YOU'RE ON!" BOBO SAID, WITH A SNEERING GRIN, "'CAUSE YOU STUTTER SO BAD, YOU'RE NEVER GONNA WIN.
YOU HAVE A MEAN STARE, LIKE THE ROCKET'S RED GLARE. IF I TELL A LITTLE JOKE YOU'LL BURST IN THE AIR.
YOU BETTER BE AWARE, I'LL FIRE ELECTRICITY.
NOW, YOU DROPPED THE CROWN 'CAUSE YOU'RE WAY TOO
J-J-JITTERY.
EVERYONE AGREES YOU'VE GOT NO ABILITY, AND I'M THE BEST. NO ONE'S GONNA BEAT ME,
BUT IF YOU DECEIVE ME, THEN I'LL CALL MY CREW, AND THEY'RE NOT GONNA BE ALL THAT *N-N-NICE* TO YOU."

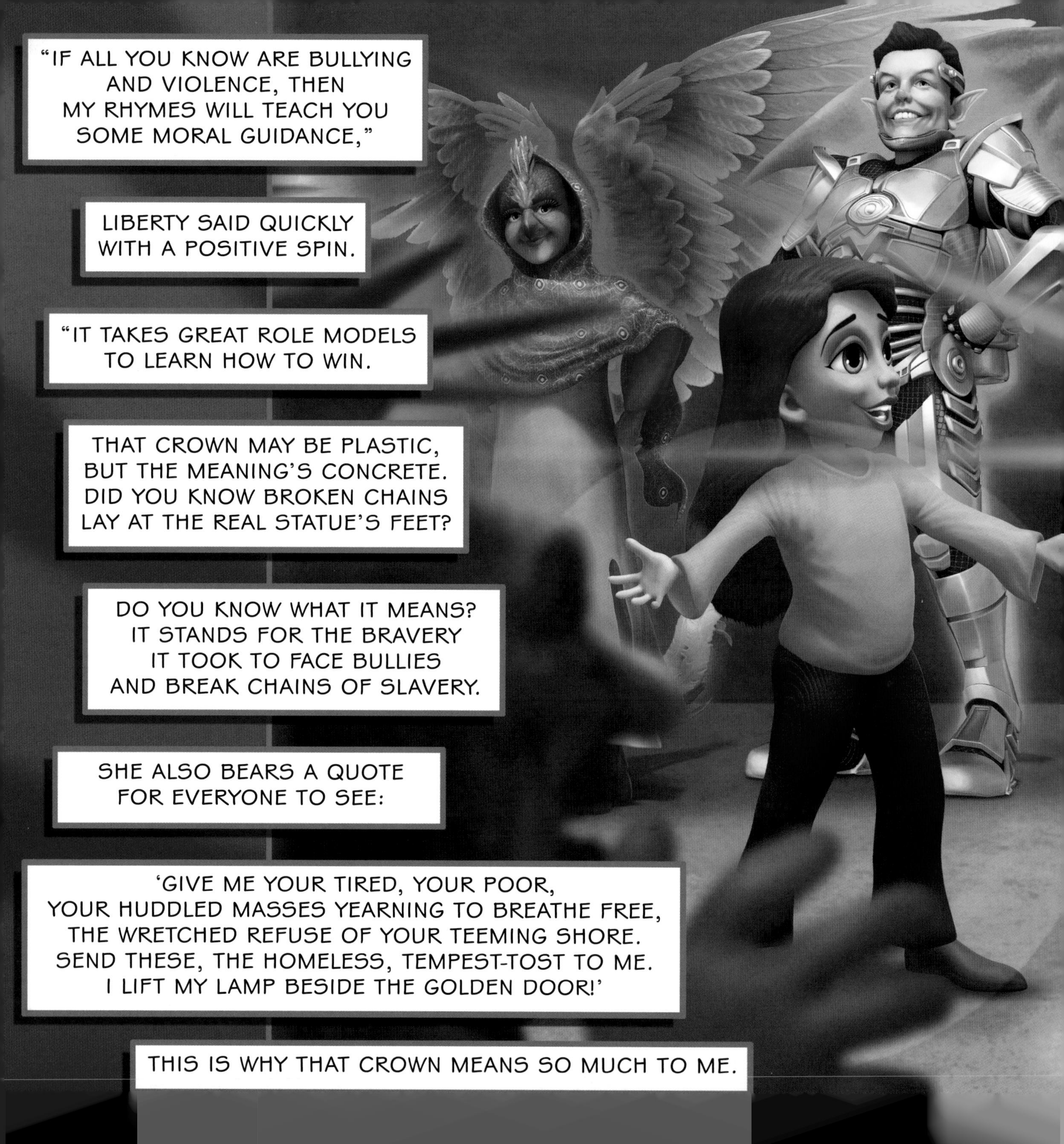
"IF ALL YOU KNOW ARE BULLYING AND VIOLENCE, THEN MY RHYMES WILL TEACH YOU SOME MORAL GUIDANCE,"
LIBERTY SAID QUICKLY WITH A POSITIVE SPIN.
"IT TAKES GREAT ROLE MODELS TO LEARN HOW TO WIN.
THAT CROWN MAY BE PLASTIC, BUT THE MEANING'S CONCRETE. DID YOU KNOW BROKEN CHAINS LAY AT THE REAL STATUE'S FEET?
DO YOU KNOW WHAT IT MEANS? IT STANDS FOR THE BRAVERY IT TOOK TO FACE BULLIES AND BREAK CHAINS OF SLAVERY.
SHE ALSO BEARS A QUOTE FOR EVERYONE TO SEE:
'GIVE ME YOUR TIRED, YOUR POOR, YOUR HUDDLED MASSES YEARNING TO BREATHE FREE, THE WRETCHED REFUSE OF YOUR TEEMING SHORE. SEND THESE, THE HOMELESS, TEMPEST-TOST TO ME. I LIFT MY LAMP BESIDE THE GOLDEN DOOR!'
THIS IS WHY THAT CROWN MEANS SO MUCH TO ME.

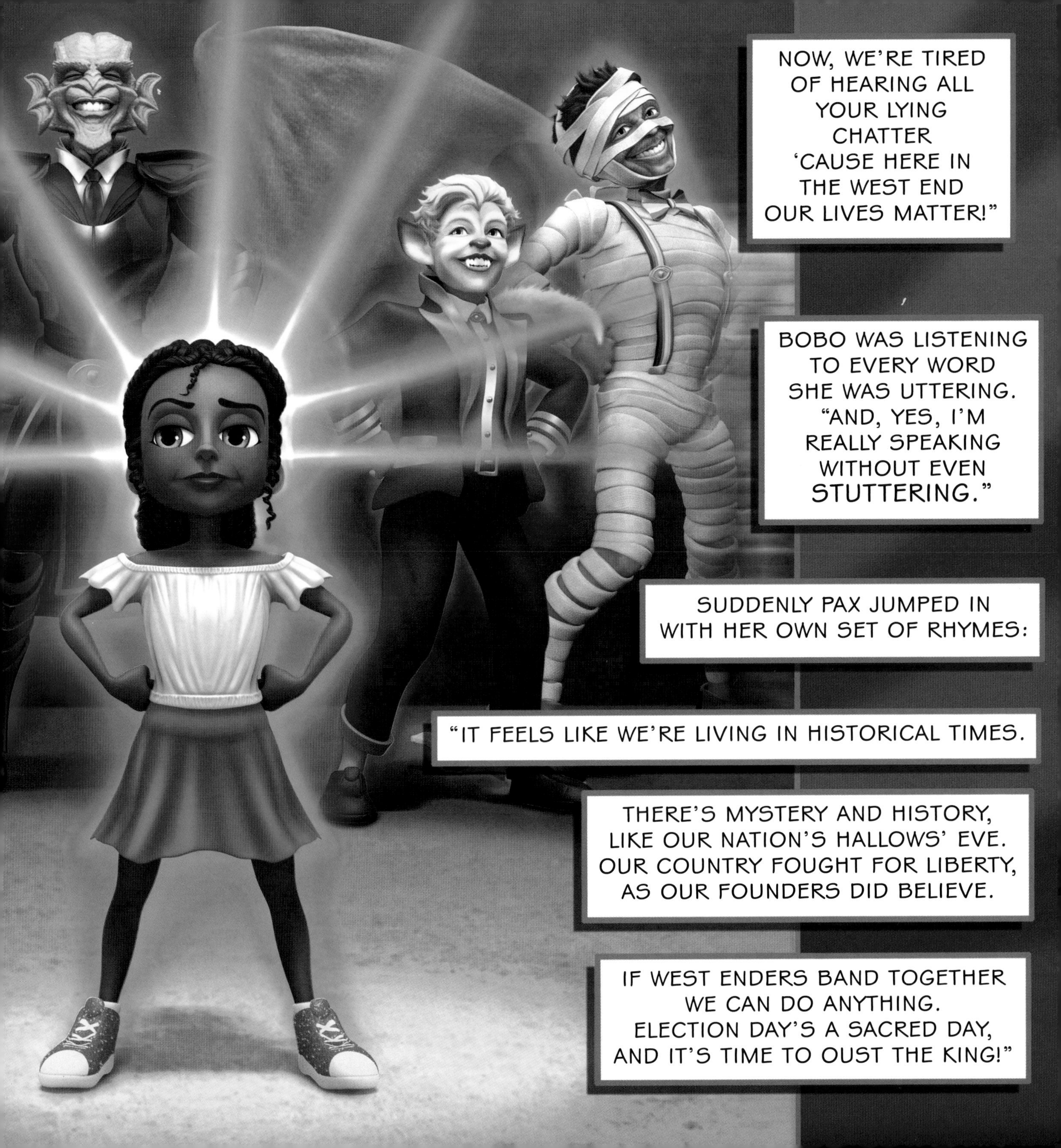
NOW, WE'RE TIRED OF HEARING ALL YOUR LYING CHATTER 'CAUSE HERE IN THE WEST END OUR LIVES MATTER!"
BOBO WAS LISTENING TO EVERY WORD SHE WAS UTTERING. "AND, YES, I'M REALLY SPEAKING WITHOUT EVEN STUTTERING."
SUDDENLY PAX JUMPED IN WITH HER OWN SET OF RHYMES:
"IT FEELS LIKE WE'RE LIVING IN HISTORICAL TIMES.
THERE'S MYSTERY AND HISTORY, LIKE OUR NATION'S HALLOWS' EVE. OUR COUNTRY FOUGHT FOR LIBERTY, AS OUR FOUNDERS DID BELIEVE.
IF WEST ENDERS BAND TOGETHER WE CAN DO ANYTHING. ELECTION DAY'S A SACRED DAY, AND IT'S TIME TO OUST THE KING!"

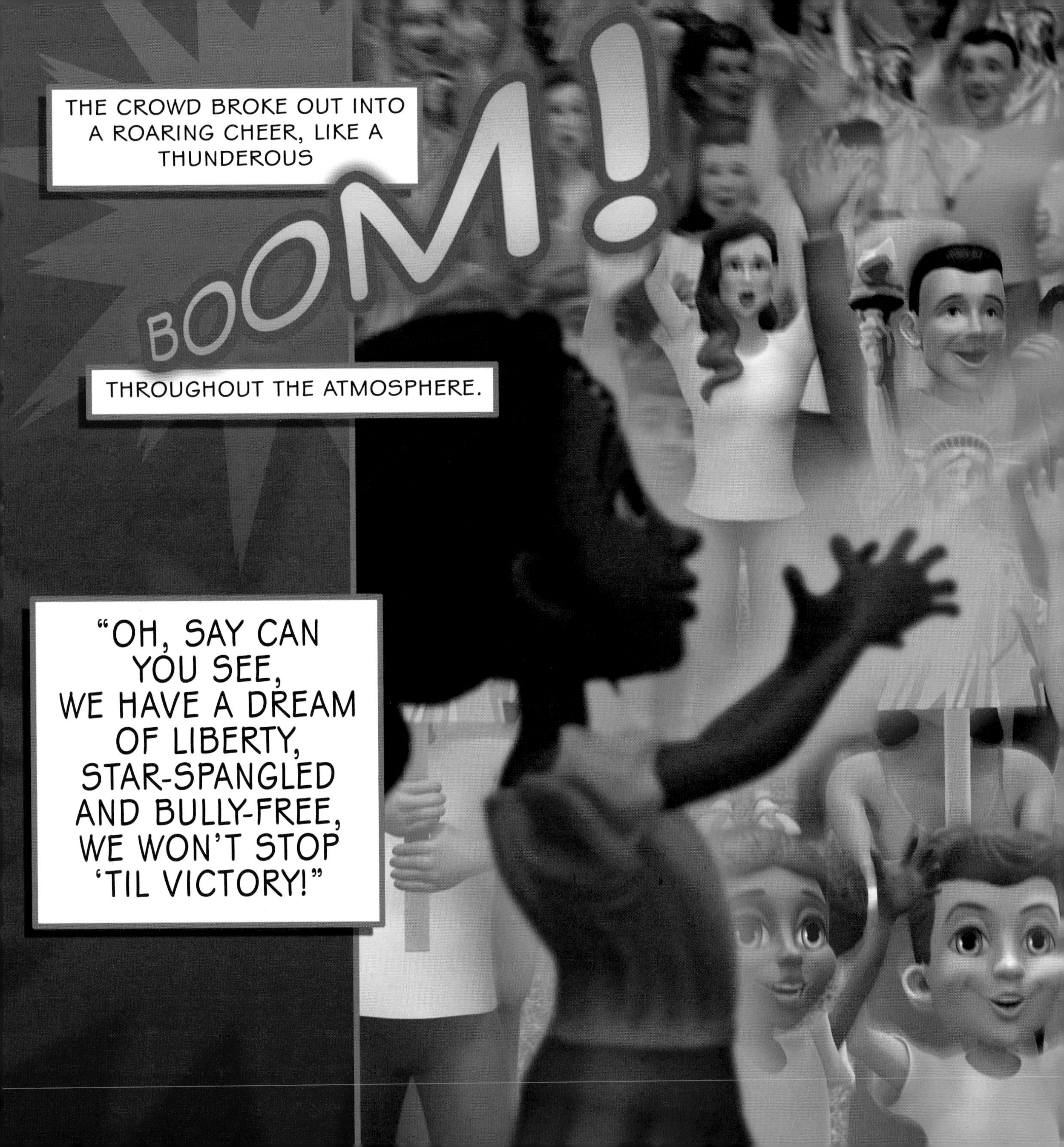
THE CROWD BROKE OUT INTO A ROARING CHEER, LIKE A THUNDEROUS
BOOM!
THROUGHOUT THE ATMOSPHERE.
"OH, SAY CAN YOU SEE, WE HAVE A DREAM OF LIBERTY, STAR-SPANGLED AND BULLY-FREE, WE WON'T STOP 'TIL VICTORY!"

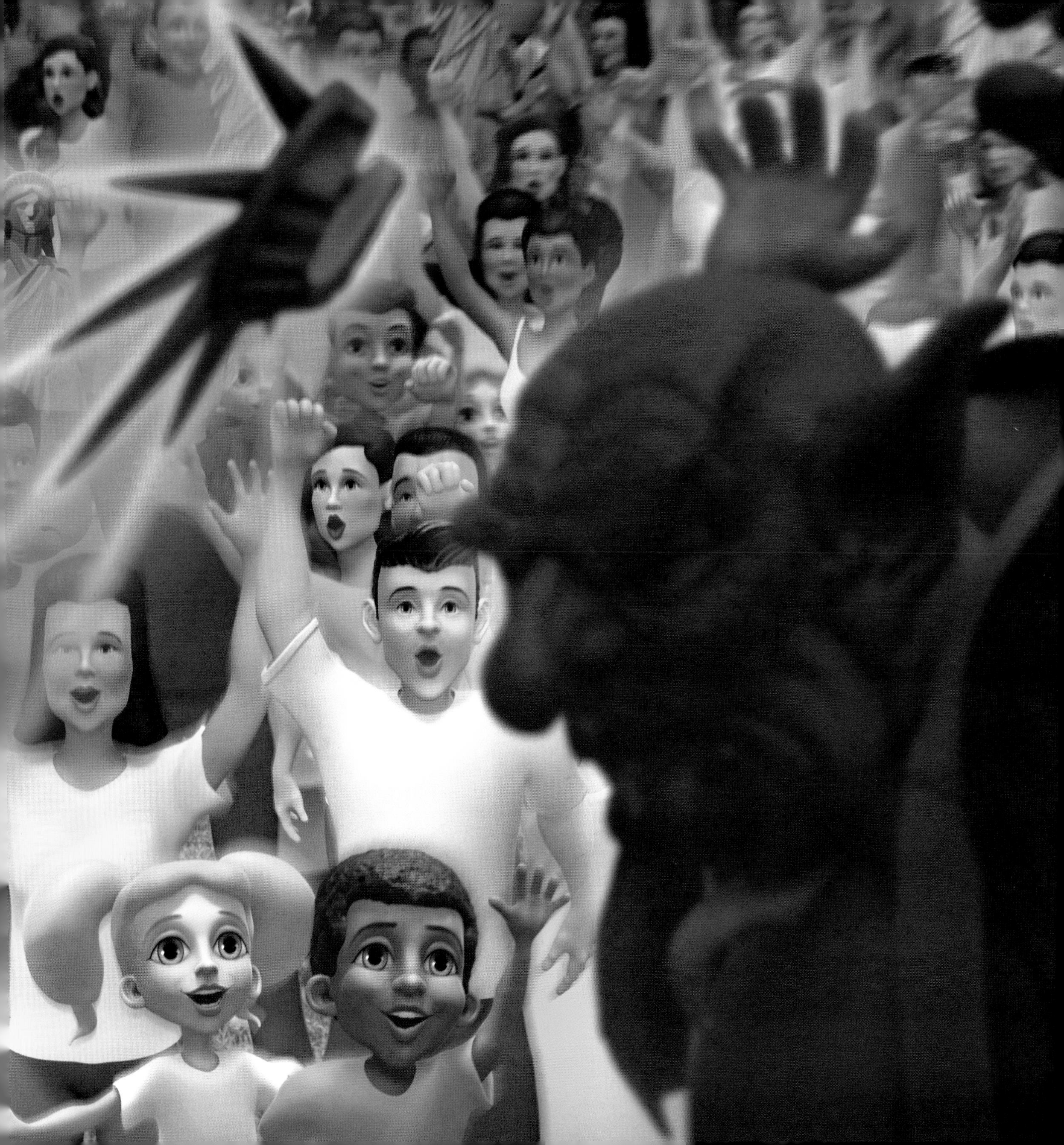

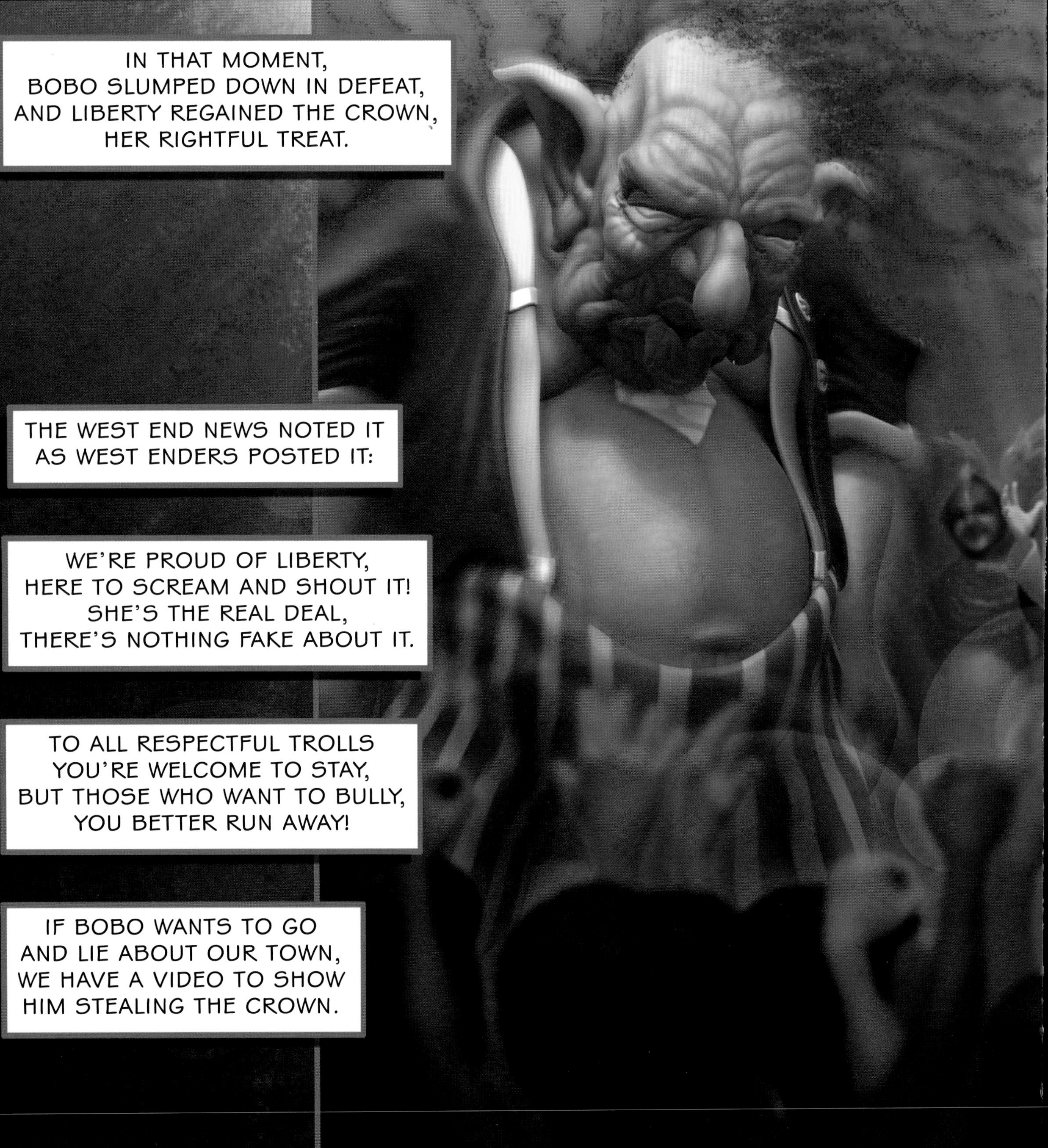
IN THAT MOMENT, BOBO SLUMPED DOWN IN DEFEAT, AND LIBERTY REGAINED THE CROWN, HER RIGHTFUL TREAT.
THE WEST END NEWS NOTED IT AS WEST ENDERS POSTED IT:
WE'RE PROUD OF LIBERTY, HERE TO SCREAM AND SHOUT IT! SHE'S THE REAL DEAL, THERE'S NOTHING FAKE ABOUT IT.
TO ALL RESPECTFUL TROLLS YOU'RE WELCOME TO STAY, BUT THOSE WHO WANT TO BULLY, YOU BETTER RUN AWAY!
IF BOBO WANTS TO GO AND LIE ABOUT OUR TOWN, WE HAVE A VIDEO TO SHOW HIM STEALING THE CROWN.

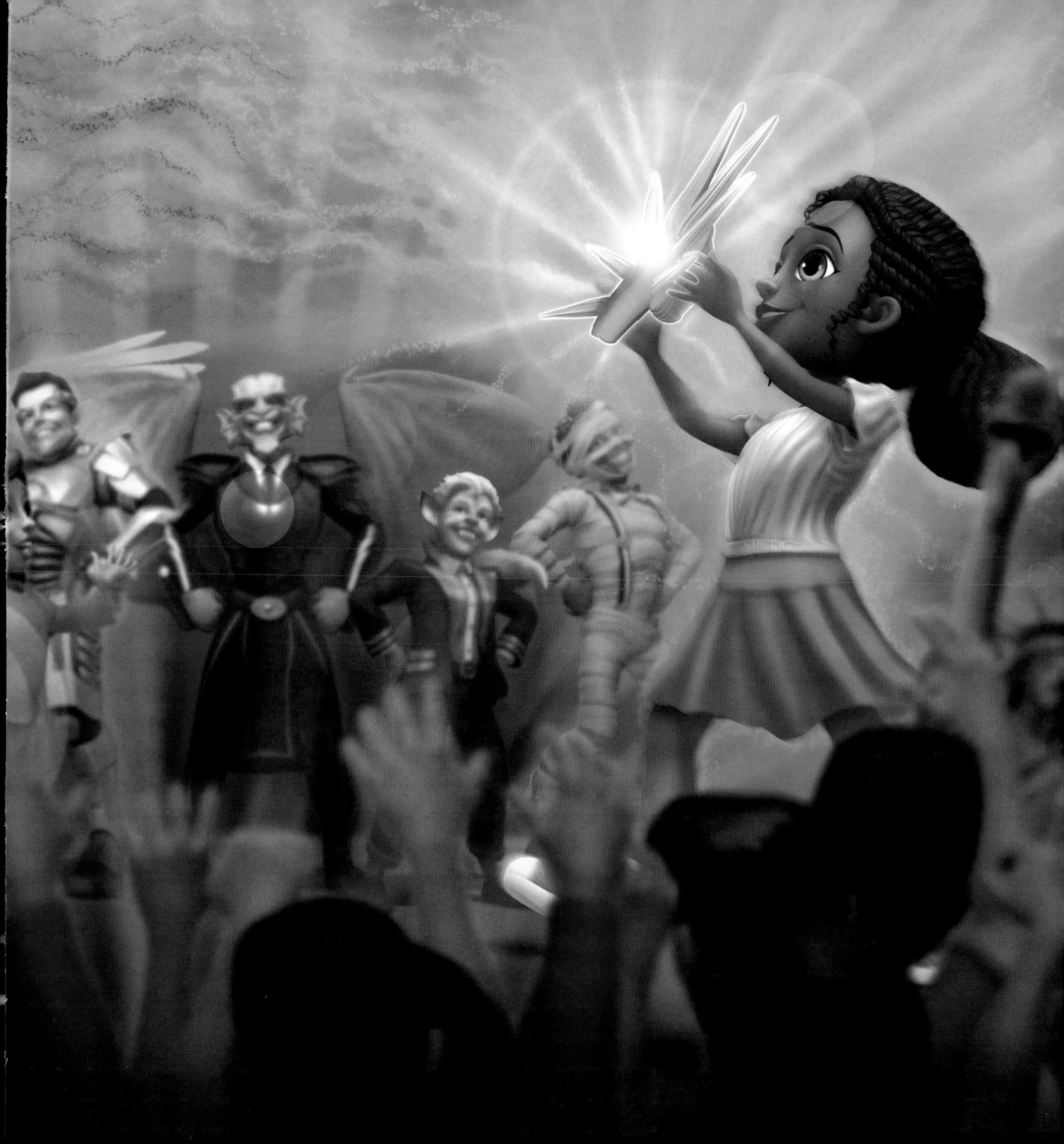

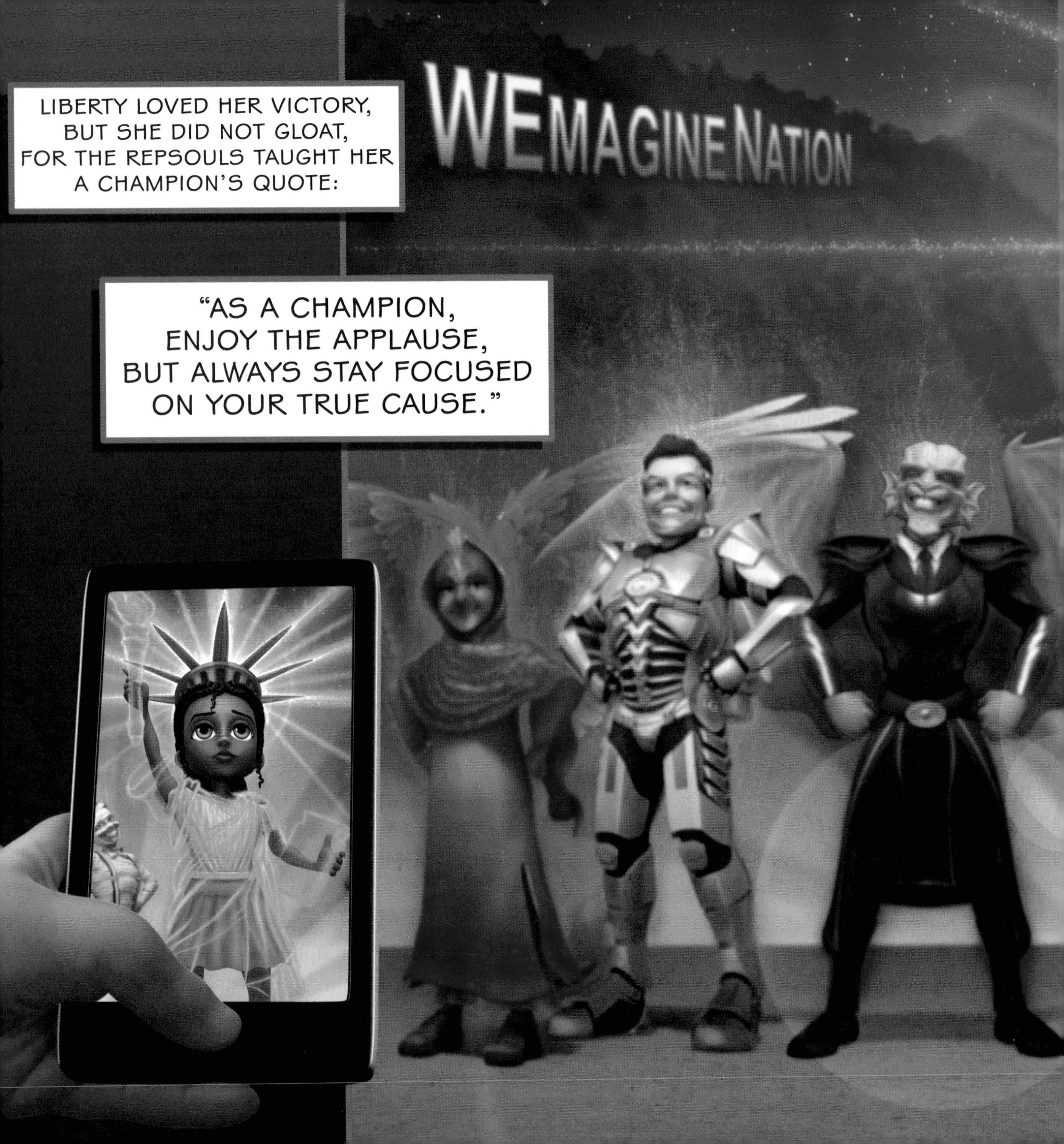
LIBERTY LOVED HER VICTORY, BUT SHE DID NOT GLOAT, FOR THE REPSOULS TAUGHT HER A CHAMPION'S QUOTE:
WEMAGINE NATION
"AS A CHAMPION, ENJOY THE APPLAUSE, BUT ALWAYS STAY FOCUSED ON YOUR TRUE CAUSE."

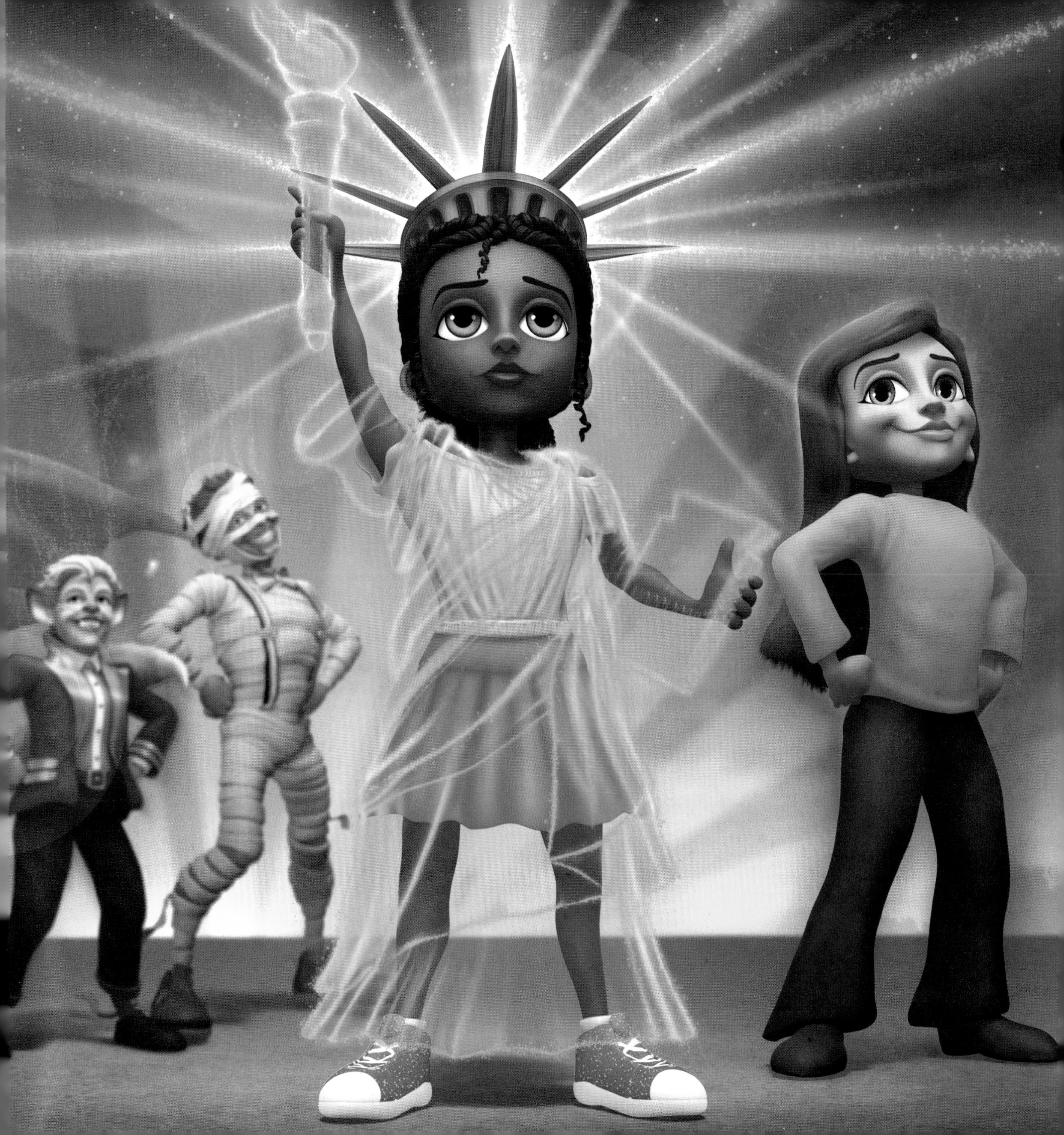

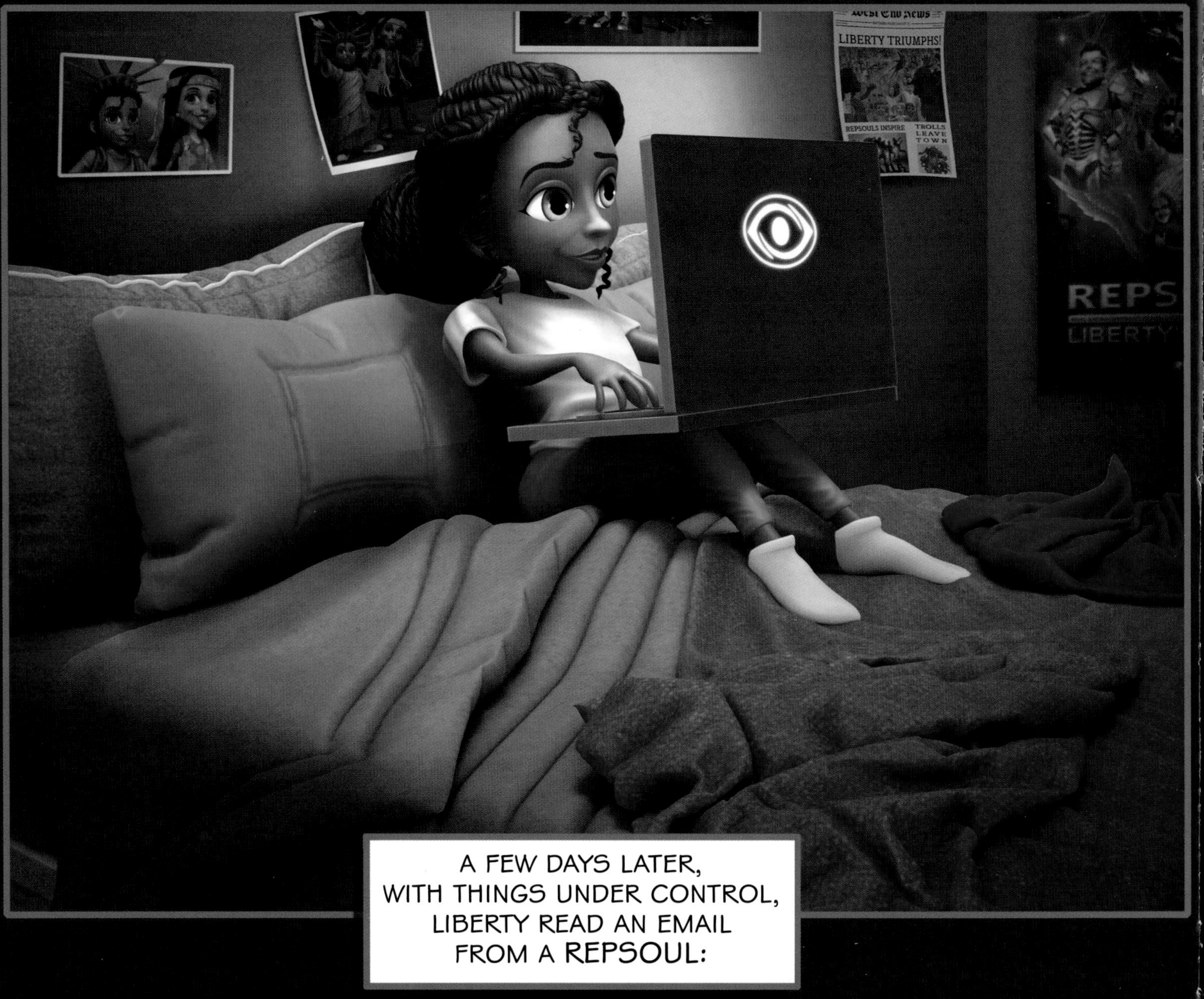

West End News
LIBERTY TRIUMPHS!
REPSOULS INSPIRE
TROLLS LEAVE TOWN
REPS
LIBERTY
A FEW DAYS LATER,
WITH THINGS UNDER CONTROL,
LIBERTY READ AN EMAIL
FROM A REPSOUL:

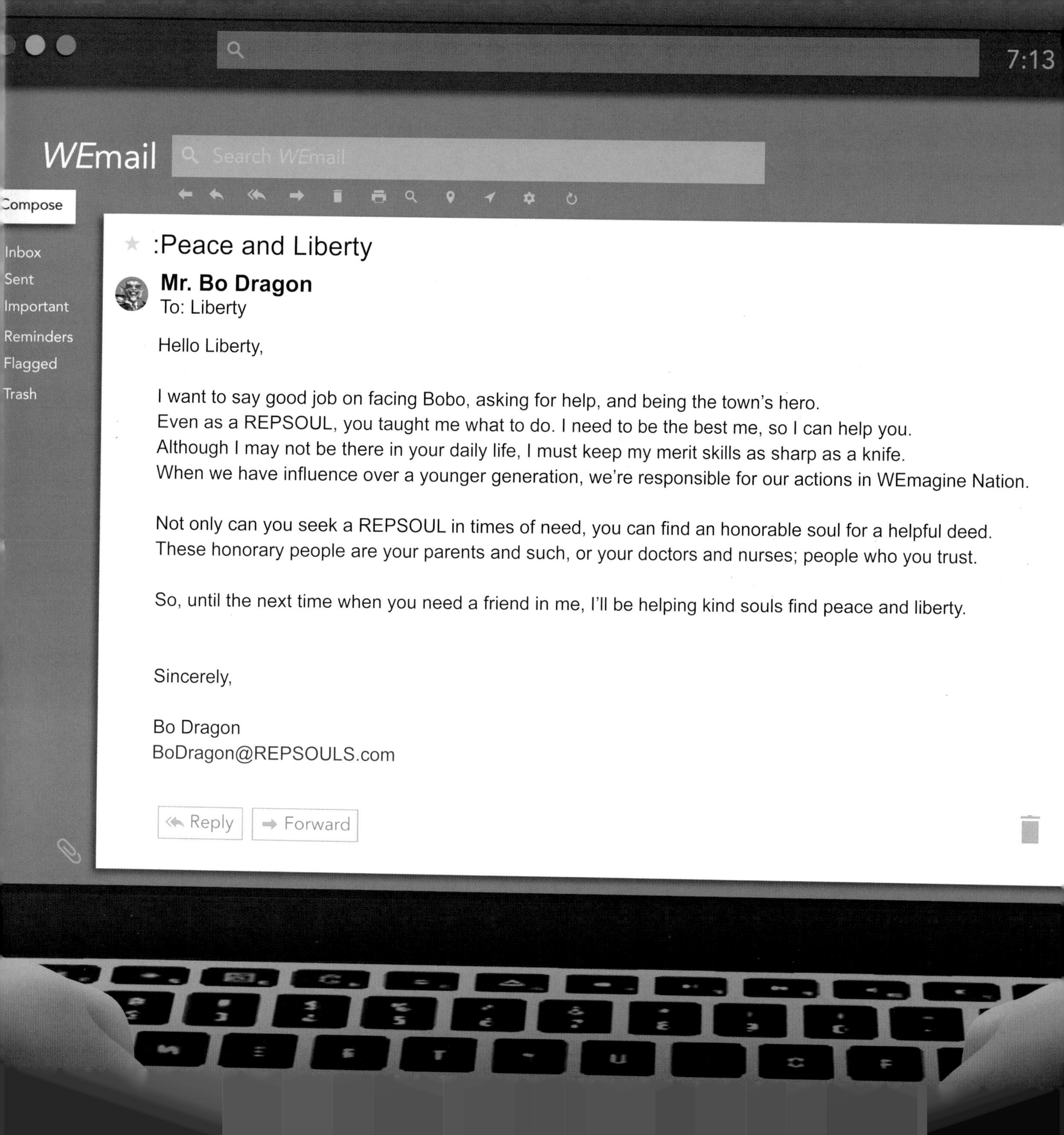
7:13
WEmail
Search WEmail
Compose
Inbox
Sent
Important
Reminders
Flagged
Trash
Reply
Forward

:Peace and Liberty

Mr. Bo Dragon
To: Liberty

Hello Liberty,

I want to say good job on facing Bobo, asking for help, and being the town's hero.
Even as a REPSOUL, you taught me what to do. I need to be the best me, so I can help you.
Although I may not be there in your daily life, I must keep my merit skills as sharp as a knife.
When we have influence over a younger generation, we're responsible for our actions in WEmagine Nation.

Not only can you seek a REPSOUL in times of need, you can find an honorable soul for a helpful deed.
These honorary people are your parents and such, or your doctors and nurses; people who you trust.

So, until the next time when you need a friend in me, I'll be helping kind souls find peace and liberty.

Sincerely,

Bo Dragon
BoDragon@REPSOULS.com

AUTHOR

ERIC GOFF BEGAN INVENTING WHIMSICAL CHARACTERS AND STORY-LINES AT A VERY YOUNG AGE, WHICH LED TO A YOUNG AUTHORS AWARD AT THE AGE OF 11. NOW, HE'S RELIVING HIS CHILDHOOD AND HONORING ROLES MODELS THROUGH THE REPSOULS SERIES.

ILLUSTRATOR

DAVE WOLF HAS BEEN DRAWING SINCE BEFORE HE CAN REMEMBER. INSPIRED BY HIS ARTISTIC FATHER, AND ENCOURAGED BY HIS LOVING MOTHER, HE PURSUED HIS PASSION BY MOVING TO SAN FRANCISCO AND STUDYING ILLUSTRATION AT THE ACADEMY OF ART. HE NOW LIVES IN SOUTHERN CALIFORNIA AND ENJOYS A WELL-ROUNDED CAREER IN ILLUSTRATION.